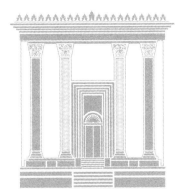

GOD-FEARERS

GENTILES & THE GOD OF ISRAEL

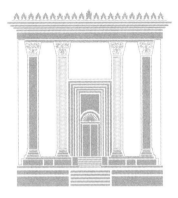

GOD-FEARERS

GENTILES & THE GOD OF ISRAEL

TOBY JANICKI

First Edition 2012
Printed in the United States of America

ISBN: 978-1-892124-65-4

First Fruits of Zion

PO Box 649, Marshfield, Missouri 65706–0649 USA
Phone (417) 468–2741, www.ffoz.org

Comments and questions: www.ffoz.org/contact

Toby Janicki is a teaching team member, staff writer, and project manager for First Fruits of Zion and Vine of David. He contributes regularly to *Messiah Journal* and has written several books in the *Mayim Chayim* series. He and his wife Shannon have four children: Aharon, Hannah, Isaac, and Abigail, and reside just outside Springfield, Missouri. Toby is a second-generation Messianic Gentile believer.

To my wife, Shannon

"A woman who fears the LORD
should be praised."

CONTENTS

INTRODUCTION

Thus says the LORD: "Stand by the roads, and look, and ask for the ancient paths, where the good way is; and walk in it, and find rest for your souls." (Jeremiah 6:16)

I'm a Gentile, but my religion is Messianic Judaism. This certainly can be confusing to some people, but I am not alone in this position. Today, scores of Gentile believers in Messiah are turning to practice Messianic Judaism as an authentic expression of faith from the time of the apostles. It has become an important reformation movement within the body of Messiah—a Jewish expression of Christianity along the lines of what the first Christians and disciples of Yeshua (Jesus) practiced nineteen centuries ago.

Modern day Messianic Judaism began to thrive during the turbulent social changes of the 1960s and 1970s. Young Jewish Christians wanted to practice discipleship to Yeshua while still maintaining their Jewish identity. It turned into a revolutionary movement that challenged many facets of institutional Christianity. For example, Messianic Judaism reopened the question of the Law and decided that, contrary to conventional theological assumptions, neither Yeshua nor his apostles intended believers to renounce the Torah of Moses. The Messianic Jewish movement does not merely look back to the past; it is prophetic in scope, looking towards the coming Messianic kingdom where Messiah will govern all of Israel according to the Torah in a restored Jerusalem.

Messianic Judaism generated a lot of excitement, not just among Jewish believers but Gentile Christians as well. If it offered a more authentic historical practice of faith in Messiah, why wouldn't non-Jewish believers also want to be part of such a revolution?

Thus, many Gentile believers, myself included, were drawn to Messianic synagogues.

But such a move raised difficult questions and controversial issues. Many Messianic Jewish leaders taught Gentile Christians that they had no place practicing the Torah's commandments and that things like the Sabbath and the dietary laws were only for the Jewish people. Instead, they encouraged non-Jewish believers to adhere to the seven universal (Noachide) laws of Judaism and remain in their churches. To me, this made little sense. The Noachide laws were incumbent upon non-Jews who had not yet experienced the revelation of Messiah and had no relationship to Israel. According to Paul, Gentiles in Yeshua are not sons of Noah but sons of Abraham.

Still others taught that Gentiles who had found Messiah were now one with the Jewish people and were either physically Israel or descended from the ten lost tribes. Adherents to these theologies insisted that Gentiles had the same relationship and obligation to the Torah that Jews did. All of this amounted to identity confusion and seemed dangerously similar to replacement theology. If Jews and Gentile believers are exactly the same, then Jewish identity for believers simply ceases to exist.

For my own part, I began to look for answers in the Apostolic Writings. Who are the Gentile believers of the book of Acts and the earliest believing communities? What was their relationship to the Jewish believers and the larger Jewish community? How did they relate to the Torah? What I discovered is that the position of Gentile believers in the apostolic community was modeled after an already-existing class of non-Jews who practiced Judaism. They were called the God-fearers. These God-fearers had a place in the synagogue and were a part of the Jewish community, not as Jews but as Gentiles among the Jewish people. If Messianic Gentiles today can recover this first-century God-fearer model, we can recover the proper biblical expression of Messianic faith as practiced by the first disciples of Yeshua. The God-fearer model resolves the difficult questions and controversial issues raised by the presence of Gentiles practicing Messianic Judaism. It defines the proper relationship between the Messianic Gentile and Messianic Jews, and it clarifies questions about Gentile observance of Torah.

Much of the content of this book was first published as a series of articles in First Fruits of Zion's *Messiah Journal*. Each article attempted to answer questions we at First Fruits of Zion were often asked in regard to the proper understanding of a Gentile believer's relationship to the Jewish people and the Torah of Moses. They were created to help wade through contentious Messianic issues such as One Law/Two House theologies, while at the same time rejecting and dispelling the notion that the Torah has no practical relevance to Gentile believers. Although this book will certainly not answer every question on this topic, I have tried to tackle the most pertinent topics. It will not be the final word on the subject of Gentile Christians and Torah, but I hope, at the very least, it is a discussion starter.

Chapter one discusses the meaning of the term Gentile and the non-Jewish believer's identity in Jesus. Chapter two explores the distinction between Jews and Gentiles in the commandments of the Torah from the perspective of the sojourner among Israel, and it also puts the "one-law" passages into context. Chapter three examines the late Second-Temple Era phenomena of scores of Gentiles participating in Judaism and attending synagogue; they were known as the God-fearers. In chapter four we examine the aspects of Torah that the apostles required new Gentile converts to observe, based on Acts 15 and the Apostolic Epistles. Finally, in chapters five, six, and seven, we take an in-depth look at a Gentile's relationship to some of the "sign commandments" of Israel: Shabbat, the festivals, tefillin, tzitzit, and mezuzah. Two appendices have been included for further study on a Gentile's relationship to Torah in rabbinic thought and the evolution of the term *ger* in the Second-Temple period.

I began my journey in Torah about fifteen years ago, and along the way I fell into many of the theological traps I am now trying to correct in this book. I offer some advice on how to avoid these traps that I myself have learned from my own mistakes. I pray that in some small way this book will aid non-Jews in Messiah who are attempting to return to the lifestyle and practice of the earliest God-fearing Gentile believers. I also hope that this book is an encouragement to my Messianic Jewish brothers and sisters. Without their commitment to the Master and their pioneering spirit, the discussions in this book would not even be on the table.

As Gentile disciples of the Master like me return to the "ancient paths" of the Messianic God-fearer, we are seeking to restore something that has been lost for almost two thousand years. May the Father guide us on our journey into the past, and allow us the grace to resurrect these truths and implement them into our lives today.

Shushan Purim 5772
Toby Janicki

CHAPTER ONE

WHAT IS A GENTILE?

────◆─◆─◆────

> When they heard these things they fell silent. And they
> glorified God, saying, "Then to the Gentiles also God has
> granted repentance that leads to life." (Acts 11:18)

A popular notion among some in the Hebrew roots movement
today is that the term "Gentile" always refers to pagans and
idolaters. This presents major identity problems for those of us
(myself included) who are Gentile by birth. We wonder, "If Gentile
means pagan, and we are not ethnically Jewish, then what should
we call ourselves? Where does that leave us?"

It doesn't help when we discover that there is even an ancient
blessing still found today in the Jewish siddur: "Blessed are You,
O LORD, our God, King of the universe, who did not make me a
Gentile."[1] If Jews are thanking God for not making them Gentiles,
why then would Gentiles in Messiah want to be labeled as such?

In this chapter we will examine the history of the term "Gentile"
in the Torah, in the rest of the Hebrew Scriptures, in Second-Temple
Judaism, and in the language of the apostles. We will discover that
the term has a variety of definitions and applications. It is not the
equivalent of the word "pagan," but in fact was the apostles' term
of choice for referring to non-Jews in Messiah.

HOLY GOYIM

In post-Biblical Hebrew the word for Gentile is *goy* (גוי, pl. *goyim*).
Marcus Jastrow's dictionary of Rabbinic Hebrew explains that *goy*
was used to refer to a "crowd, nation, people, gentile," and was even

a designation for an "idolater."[2] However, in Biblical Hebrew—that is, in the Tanach—its primary definition is "nation" or "people."[3] For example, we find it used this way in its first biblical occurrence:

> From these the coastland peoples [*goyim*] spread in their lands, each with his own language, by their clans, in their nations [*goyim*]. (Genesis 10:5)

Genesis uses it to describe both Abraham's offspring—"I will make of you a great nation (*goy*)" (Genesis 12:2)—and Ishmael's— "I will make him into a great nation (*goy*)" (Genesis 17:20).[4] In fact the nation of Israel is called a *goy* in the Torah. One of the strongest examples of this is found in Exodus 19:6:

> And you shall be to me a kingdom of priests and a holy nation [*goy*]. These are the words that you shall speak to the people of Israel.[5]

Here, Israel is literally called a "holy *goy*." This shows that, in Biblical Hebrew, the word "*goy*" implies no disparagement or condescension. Even in the rebuke of the prophets, it simply means "nation" or "people."

> Behold, I am bringing against you a nation [*goy*] from afar, O house of Israel, declares the LORD. It is an enduring nation [*goy*]; it is an ancient nation [*goy*], a nation [*goy*] whose language you do not know, nor can you understand what they say. (Jeremiah 5:15)

Clements, in the *Theological Dictionary of the Old Testament*, comments on the use of *goy* at the close of the biblical period:

> In a usage in which Israel could declare itself as a goy, there was clearly no possibility of the term taking on a completely hostile religious meaning, although development in this direction does begin to emerge.[6]

TRANSITION PERIOD

One of the definitions for *goy* in rabbinic Hebrew is "idolater," a connotation that began to emerge during the intertestamental period. Even though the Torah uses *goy* to describe Israel as a nation, later books of the Tanach developed a preference for *am* ("nation," עם) and *mishpachah* ("family," משפחה) over *goy*. One of the contributing factors to this was that after the Babylonian captivity, Israel was no longer a *goy* in the sense of a political or territorial entity. Clements comments again:

> The tendency to regard the non-Israelite nations adversely on account of their religion, combined with Israel's own political misfortunes, lent a distinctive coloring to the term goyim. When this is viewed in conjunction with the preference found in the OT for Israel to describe itself as *'am*, "people," and a *mishpachah*, "family," rather than a goy, in view of the political overtones of the latter term, it is not difficult to see how the ground was prepared for the later Talmudic usage in which goy and goyim took on a specific and adverse meaning.[7]

During the late Second-Temple period, the Jewish community interpreted the prohibition on marriage to the Canaanite nations in Deuteronomy 7:1–4 as including all Gentile nations.[8] Justifiably, Jews began to regard themselves as the sole proprietors of monotheism. Therefore, they associated the other nations (*goyim*) with idolatry.

DOGS AND SWINE

Our Master had limited contact with non-Jews. He shared common rabbinic attitudes towards them. In the Talmud there is a specific prohibition on teaching idolaters Torah.[9]

Yeshua seems to have been of a similar persuasion in Matthew 7:6:

> Do not give dogs what is holy, and do not throw your pearls before pigs, lest they trample them underfoot and turn to attack you.

Samuel Lachs points out that "pearls" and "what is holy" refers to teachings of Torah,[10] and additionally "dogs" and "pigs" appear in rabbinic literature as referring to Samaritans and Gentiles.[11]

Lachs suggests that the sentiment behind Yeshua's dogs-and-pigs saying is the rabbinic prohibition on teaching Torah to Gentiles.[12]

The Master appears to continue these sentiments in dealing with the Gentile Syrophoenician woman: "It is not right to take the children's bread and throw it to the dogs." (Matthew 15:26). Once again he compares a Gentile to a dog.[13] C.S. Lewis takes note of the brash reply to this Gentile woman:

> I think to myself that the shocking reply to the Syrophoe-nician woman (it came alright in the end) is to remind all us Gentile Christians—who forget it easily enough or flirt with anti-Semitism—that the Hebrews are spiritu-ally senior to us, that God did entrust the descendants of Abraham with the first revelation of Himself.[14]

Gentiles may feel disoriented by passages like these, but the Master's words must be balanced against the full context of his vision for the Gentile nations.[15]

THE MISSION TO THE GENTILES

While he was among us, Yeshua focused his mission specifically on the House of Israel, i.e., the Jewish people.

> These twelve Jesus sent out, instructing them, "Go nowhere among the Gentiles and enter no town of the Samaritans, but go rather to the lost sheep of the house of Israel." (Matthew 10:5–6)

God made his covenant with Israel, not with the nations. Outside of Israel, Gentiles have no relation to God's promises and covenants. The book of Hebrews reiterates the exclusive province of the New Covenant by quoting Jeremiah 31:31–32:

> Behold, the days are coming, declares the Lord, when I will establish a new covenant with the house of Israel and with the house of Judah ... For this is the covenant that I will make with the house of Israel after those days, declares the Lord ... they shall be my people. (Hebrews 8:8–10)

If the nations were going to find a place at the table of God, it would have to be done within the context of the family of Israel. This would come through the Messiah. Even from his birth, Yeshua was promised to be "a light for revelation to the Gentiles."[16] Before leaving his disciples, he revealed his plan to bring the nations to the Father through himself:

> Go therefore and make disciples of all nations, baptizing them in the name of the Father and of the Son and of the Holy Spirit, teaching them to observe all that I have commanded you. And behold, I am with you always, to the end of the age. (Matthew 28:19–20)

Yeshua called his Jewish disciples to deliver his teachings to the Gentiles of the world. Additionally, he called upon them to immerse the Gentiles, corresponding to the Jewish practice of *tevilah* ("ritual immersion," טבילה).[17] Note that, in rabbinic law, Gentiles did not receive immersion except upon conversion. There is an interesting discussion in the Talmud about what constitutes a full proselyte:

> Our Rabbis taught: "If a proselyte was circumcised but had not performed the prescribed ritual ablution, R. Eliezer said, 'Behold he is a proper proselyte; for so we find that our forefathers were circumcised and had not performed ritual ablution.' If he performed the prescribed ablution but had not been circumcised, R. Joshua said, 'Behold he is a proper proselyte; for so we find that the mothers had performed ritual immersion but had not been circumcised.'" (b. *Yevamot* 46a)

At the end of the discussion, the sages ruled that one must have both circumcision and immersion to be considered a legal convert. Nevertheless, this passage records an opinion to the effect that one only had to be immersed. (This stands to reason, since circumcision only applies to half of the human species.) In light of this discussion, Matthew 28 should be understood to indicate that a Gentile immersed in Messiah attains a status different from that of one outside of Messiah (i.e., different from that of a modern-day Noachide or first-century God-fearer).[18] While not a formal, legal conversion in the halachic sense, the immersion does indicate that some type of conversion has taken place. Immersion always signified a change of status and most often a change from unclean to clean. Jonathan Draper finds in the Jewish-Christian writings of the *Didache* a sort of initiation/inclusion meal for Gentiles who have come to Messiah and have been immersed.[19] The Gentile immersed in Messiah is purified and has undergone a change of legal status.

PETER'S VISION

The transformation and purification of the Gentile believer in Messiah is illustrated in the story of Peter's vision in Acts 10. An issue for Jew-Gentile relations in the days of the apostles was the uncleanness of Gentile dwellings. According to some strict interpretations of Pharisaic purity laws, entering the home of a Gentile incurred Levitical impurity. Eating in a Gentile's house defiled the food.[20] Although the full reason for and history of this prohibition is a bit obscure, it probably related to ritual impurity, idolatry, food issues, and a general fear that Jewish people would be led astray if they fellowshipped in Gentile houses. Following his trip to Cornelius' house, Peter proclaimed to his Jewish brothers:

> "As I began to speak, the Holy Spirit fell on them just as on us at the beginning …" And they glorified God, saying, "Then to the Gentiles also God has granted repentance that leads to life." (Acts 11:15–18)

> "You yourselves know how unlawful it is for a Jew to associate with or to visit anyone of another nation, but God has shown me that I should not call any person common or unclean … Truly I understand that God shows no partiality, but in every nation anyone who fears him and does what is right is acceptable to him." (Acts 10:28, 34–35)

Peter oversaw the immersion of Cornelius and the other Gentiles present (Acts 10:48) and he ate with them (Acts 11:2–3). As both a God-fearer and a believer in Messiah, Cornelius was no longer considered an idolater and unclean. He was to be received into full fellowship with the believing Jewish community.[21] He had repented and turned to the God of Israel and his only son Yeshua, and he was now purified from idolatry by faith.

Peter's experience with Cornelius is retold throughout the book of Acts. The anecdote serves as a *ma'aseh* (מעשה), i.e., an incident that serves as a a basis for a halachic ruling. This *ma'aseh* permitted entering the houses of and eating with the uncircumcised believers in Yeshua.[22] Peter was the Master's chief disciple; therefore his behavior carried enormous weight for the believers in Jerusalem.[23] If he did something, his reputation was so strong that it could be considered as permitted. Peter later cited his *ma'aseh* of the cleansing of Gentiles in Messiah to the Jerusalem Council, and a subsequent ruling was passed by James and the elders over the community.[24]

STILL GENTILES?

According to the Jerusalem Council (Acts 15), Gentiles have full access to God and his covenants through Yeshua without the need of formal conversion. In a sense, through Messiah, God has redeemed the term "Gentile." But should they still be called Gentiles?

The Greek word commonly translated as "Gentiles" in the Gospels and Epistles is the word *ethnos* (εθνος). Septuagint Greek uses the term *ethnos* to translate both *am* ("nation") and *goy* ("gentile").[25] It is up to the translator to decide which word the context dictates, and in this book we will follow the standards of the English Standard Version.

Ethnos has a semantic value equivalent to the English word "ethnicity." Therefore, when reading "Gentile," in the New Testament it should be seen as a synonym for "ethnicity."

Karl Schmidt points out that the New Testament sometimes uses the term Gentile in the sense of "pagan" and sometimes merely as a designation for believers or monotheists who are non-Jewish.[26] For example, the apostles at times used the term Gentile as an equivalent for heathen idolaters:

> Not in the passion of lust like the Gentiles who do not know God. (1 Thessalonians 4:5)

> The time that is past suffices for doing what the Gentiles want to do, living in sensuality, passions, drunkenness, orgies, drinking parties, and lawless idolatry. (1 Peter 4:3)[27]

Yet Paul also uses the term to designate non-Jews who have come to know Messiah:

> To the brothers who are of the Gentiles in Antioch and Syria. (Acts 15:23)

> This mystery is that the Gentiles are fellow heirs, members of the same body, and partakers of the promise in Christ Jesus through the gospel. (Ephesians 3:6)

> For this reason I, Paul, a prisoner for Christ Jesus on behalf of you Gentiles. (Ephesians 3:1)[28]

In apostolic vernacular, Gentiles are still called Gentiles even after coming to Messiah, yet at the same time the connotation of "pagan" is sometimes retained in the context. This creates a difficult dichotomy in definition, but it is one with which the apostles were comfortable operating. The bigger issue, for Paul at least, was the spiritual state of the individual.

SPIRITUAL CONVERSION

In Colossians 2:11–12, Paul describes the technical process of conversion (i.e., circumcision and immersion) in spiritual terms. This conversion is not accomplished by human hands but by faith in God: "In him also you were circumcised with a circumcision made without hands ... the circumcision of Christ." Commenting on Paul's words in Ephesians 2:19 that Gentiles in Messiah are "no longer strangers and aliens," Rabbi Lichtenstein states, "For now they were complete proselytes through faith in the righteous Messiah."[29]

In Judaism, a formal convert is called *ben Avraham* ("son of Abraham," בן אברהם) or *bat Avraham* ("daughter of Abraham," בת אברהם), respectively.[30] This is precisely the language that Paul uses to describe new Gentile believers. He tells them they are now "sons of Abraham" (Galatians 3:7), and when addressing the mixed congregation in Corinth, he even refers to the Israelites that came out of Egypt as "our fathers" (1 Corinthians 10:1).[31] This indicates that the Patriarchs and the Exodus from Egypt have now become a part of the Gentile believer's spiritual heritage.

Paul continues on this theme of spiritual conversion in Romans:

> If a man who is uncircumcised keeps the precepts of the law, will not his uncircumcision be regarded as circumcision? … circumcision is a matter of the heart, by the Spirit. (Romans 2:26, 29)

In Yeshua, the uncircumcised (i.e., Gentile) becomes inwardly circumcised (i.e., inwardly Jewish), but this in no way makes Gentile believers Jewish in the flesh, i.e., physically or legally. Nor does it diminish the legal and practical distinctions between a Jewish person and a Gentile believer. The apostles never referred to the Gentile believers as Jews or Israelites. In Romans 3, Paul contrasts the respective role of Gentile believers with that of the Jewish people, emphasizing the uniqueness of the Jewish people: "Then what advantage has the Jew? Or what is the value of circumcision? Much in every way. To begin with, the Jews were entrusted with the oracles of God" (Romans 3:1–2).

He ends the same chapter by constructing a short midrash on the Shema ("Hear, O Israel: The LORD our God, the LORD is one"—Deuteronomy 6:4).[32] He writes:

> Is God the God of Jews only? Is he not the God of Gentiles also? Yes, of Gentiles also, since God is one. (Romans 3:29)

In other words if God is truly One then he is the God of both Jews and Gentiles. To eliminate that distinction is to trample on the central creed of Judaism, and to do that is to limit God.

THE EXTENSION OF SALVATION

God expresses his love of humanity by extending salvation to those outside Israel and drawing them into his family. Those of us from the nations should be proud to be Gentile. God has created us as Gentiles. The gathering of the nations is a fulfillment of Messiah's death on the cross, and salvation can now be found by anyone who will turn to him.

The word "Gentile" is not a negative term, nor does it refer to idolaters in any essential way. However, remember what we pointed out: The term Gentile does not even appear in the Greek text of the New Testament. Rather, the word *ethnos* is used which is then translated into English as "Gentile." *Ethnos* means "ethnicity" and does not mean idolater. The very fact that non-Jews are still called *ethnos* after coming to Messiah proves that their ethnicity has not been changed and they remain as one from the nations.

Although the term Gentile has had various implications in different contexts, its primary meaning is that of "one from the nations." This is the designation that the apostles used to distinguish non-Jewish believers from Jewish believers. If it was good enough for them, it should be good enough for us. However, we should always bear in mind that a Gentile in Messiah is not the same legally or spiritually as one outside of Messiah. Gentiles in Messiah have been purified and brought into the "commonwealth of Israel" (Ephesians 2:12).

My colleagues at First Fruits of Zion have created an alternate blessing for Gentile believers to recite in place of the standard "who has not made me a Gentile"; it is this: "Blessed are You, O LORD, our God, King of the universe, who has given even to Gentiles the repentance to life." This blessing is based on the one uttered by the apostles in Jerusalem after Peter reiterated to them the miraculous outpouring of the Holy Spirit upon the Gentiles. In Acts 11:18 it says that upon hearing the news "they glorified God, saying, 'Then to the Gentiles also God has granted repentance that leads to life.'" "They glorified God" is a term often used in the New Testament for pronouncing a blessing.[33] Gentile believers can recite this blessing with pride and assurance that they, like their Jewish brethren, have been made according to the Father's divine will.

Gentiles in Messiah have been transformed by Yeshua's redeeming work and, as we shall see, are more than just mere Noachides or first-century God-fearers. Those of us from the nations should be proud of who God created us to be. We have an important opportunity to be a light for HaShem and his kingdom that only we can be. Together with our Jewish brothers and sisters in Messiah, we must work towards establishing Messiah's kingdom and the rule of Torah, while at the same time accepting our own unique roles.

At the same time, some may wonder whether it matters if a person is called a Jew or a Gentile. Aren't we all one new man in Messiah? Doesn't the Torah say that there shall be one law for both the stranger and the native-born alike? In the next chapter, we will consider the context of those passages that seem to apply the same standard and obligation of Torah-law to both Jews and Gentile believers.

CHAPTER TWO

ONE LAW FOR ALL

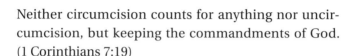

> Neither circumcision counts for anything nor uncir-
> cumcision, but keeping the commandments of God.
> (1 Corinthians 7:19)

In the previous chapter, we have established the unique and important role of Gentiles in Messiah. We are ready to begin examining the Gentiles' relationship to Judaism and the Torah of Moses. First off, we must realize that the Torah has different instructions for different people within the commonwealth of Israel. To say that God's Torah is still in force today has vastly different implications depending upon who you are. This realization will affect the way we read the Bible, in particular the New Testament, and will help put the Scriptures back in their proper context, especially when it comes to the distinction between Jews and Gentiles.

DISTINCTIONS IN THE TORAH

When we speak about how much of the Torah various individuals, be they Jew, Gentile, priest, or Levite, are obligated to observe, it is important to point out that no one person is obligated to observe the entire 613 commandments of the Torah. Some individuals are obligated to observe more commandments than others, but no one is obligated or even permitted to observe them all.

When the Torah introduces a commandment, it usually specifies carefully to whom the commandments are addressed. For example, we find the oft-repeated phrase, "Command to Aaron and his sons, saying …" referring specifically to instructions for priests. Even within the priesthood, some men are excluded from various commandments based upon physical defects.[34] Some commandments apply only to the Levites, and some apply only to certain families within the House of Levi, such as the various duties associated with transporting the Tabernacle.[35] There are also instructions that obviously only apply to men and those that only apply to women. A good example of this would be the bodily-purity regulations of Leviticus 12 and 15. All of these distinctions and various levels of obligations are not based upon personal merit or right standing within the community but strictly upon lineage and gender.

Because of these inherent distinctions, rabbinic literature speaks of the study and observance of Torah assuming that certain commandments are incumbent on some groups but not upon others. The commandments must be viewed within the context of whom they are addressing. This is most clearly exposed amidst discussions regarding the relationship between non-Jews and the Torah.

> Rabbi Meir used to say, "Whence do we know that even a heathen who studies the Torah is as a High Priest? From the verse, '[You shall therefore keep my statutes, and my judgments:] which, if man do, he shall live in them' [Leviticus 18:5]. Priests, Levites, and Israelites are not mentioned, but men: hence thou mayest learn that even a heathen who studies the Torah is as a High Priest!"—That refers to their own seven laws. (b.*Sanhedrin* 59a)

Notice the clarifying last sentence. According to the Gemara, when Rabbi Meir speaks of a Gentile studying and observing Torah, he is not speaking of a Gentile keeping the Torah in the same way as an Israelite. Rather the Gentile observes the commandments which (in his mind) apply to a Gentile. Therefore, in Talmudic thought, to say that a Gentile keeps Torah is different from saying that a Jew keeps Torah. But does the Torah itself really make such a distinction between Jews and Gentiles as it does with priests, Levites, men, and women?

THE STRANGER AMONG YOU

The rabbis derive commandments applicable to all nations from the Noah story in Genesis. Noah, of course, appears on the scene before Abraham, the father of the Hebrew nation, and therefore is seen as a prototype of the righteous non-Jew. Once Noah steps off the ark, God gives him specific instructions:

> Be fruitful and multiply and fill the earth … Every moving thing that lives shall be food for you. And as I gave you the green plants, I give you everything. But you shall not eat flesh with its life, that is, its blood. And for your lifeblood I will require a reckoning: from every beast I will require it and from man. From his fellow man I will require a reckoning for the life of man. Whoever sheds the blood of man, by man shall his blood be shed, for God made man in his own image. (Genesis 9:1–6)

These instructions were then codified by the sages of Israel into what is known as the seven laws of Noah or Noachide Laws: the prohibitions against idolatry, murder, theft, sexual immorality, blasphemy, and eating a limb from a live animal as well as the injunction to set up courts.[36] The commandments given to Noah are an important place to begin when discussing a non-Jew's obligation to the Torah, but a better place to gain a more detailed perspective on Jew/Gentile distinction is the Torah concept of the *ger* (גר).

Ger is usually translated as "stranger" or "sojourner." When used in contrast to the children of Israel, it refers to the non-Israelites who are dwelling and sojourning among the people. The *ger* might be a casual passerby or a Gentile family who make their permanent home within the land of Israel. The *ger* did not become an official "son of Israel," but rather chose, for various reasons, to cast his lot with the people of Israel. Non-Jews first appear among Israel during the Exodus where they voluntarily choose to leave Egypt as companions of the Jewish people.[37]

In many other economies of the ancient Near East, strangers did not have the same civil rights and protections as the native population. The strangers in Israel, however, enjoyed the Torah's protection, which included being provided with various forms of charity and rest from servitude on the Sabbath.[38] Just because they could not defend themselves did not mean that they should be abused. Commandments regarding proper behavior toward the stranger are some of the most ubiquitous in the Torah.

> You shall not oppress a hired servant who is poor and needy, whether he is one of your brothers or one of the sojourners [*ger*] who are in your land within your towns. You shall give him his wages on the same day, before the sun sets (for he is poor and counts on it), lest he cry against you to the LORD, and you be guilty of sin. (Deuteronomy 24:14–15)

By the time of the late Second-Temple period it was almost universally accepted that the term *ger* referred to a proselyte; in others words, one who had made a formal conversion to Judaism and was no longer considered a Gentile.[39] Proselytes fell under full obligation to keep the Torah in the same manner as any Jew, and this is most likely how the apostles would have interpreted many of the laws about the *ger* as well.[40] But for now we will examine the concept of the *ger* from a literal, contextual, *sola scriptura* view, as is understood by most Protestant Bible scholars today, i.e., that of the non-Jewish sojourner.

THE STRANGER AND PASSOVER[41]

The first example we find of a *ger*'s unique relationship to the Torah is in regard to the instructions about the Passover sacrifice. A close reading of this passage reveals that the Torah does distinguish between the obligations of an Israelite and those of the stranger.

> And the LORD said to Moses and Aaron, "This is the statute of the Passover: no foreigner shall eat of it, but every slave that is bought for money may eat of it after you have circumcised him. No foreigner or hired servant may eat of it. It shall be eaten in one house; you shall not take any of the flesh outside the house, and you shall not break any of its bones. All the congregation of Israel shall keep it. If a stranger [ger] shall sojourn with you and would keep the Passover to the LORD, let all his males be circumcised. Then he may come near and keep it; he

shall be as a native of the land. But no uncircumcised person shall eat of it." (Exodus 12:43–48)

Biblical commentator Nahum Sarna explains that the non-Israelite "was not required to celebrate the Passover; but if he desired to do so [by sacrificing a Passover lamb], and thus identify himself and his family with the national experience of Israel, he had to first submit to circumcision."[42] The *ger* is permitted to participate in the Passover sacrifice if he is circumcised, but, unlike the native-born Israelite, he is in no way obligated to do so.

However, elsewhere we read that unlike with the sacrifice, a Gentile sojourning among Israel was not permitted to have any leaven in his dwellings.

> For seven days no leaven is to be found in your houses. If anyone eats what is leavened, that person will be cut off from the congregation of Israel, whether he is a sojourner [*ger*] or a native of the land. (Exodus 12:19)[43]

No leaven was to be found in Israel during the entire week of Unleavened Bread, either in the dwellings of the native born or the *ger*. Nevertheless a distinction remains in regard to the obligation of the actual Passover sacrifice.

The Passover sacrifice section in Exodus 12 continues with a curious verse:

> There shall be one law [*torah achat,* תורה אחת] for the native and for the stranger [*ger*] who sojourns among you." (Exodus 12: 49)

What about the phrase, "There shall be one law"? Does this contradict the idea that the non-Israelite has a choice? When this last verse is read alone, it may give the impression that all of the Torah's commands apply equally for both the *ger* and for the native. It is tempting to remove that verse from its context and read "one law" as if it refers to the entire scope of the Torah. However, in the context of the Passover sacrifice we can see that it is not meant in this way. Exodus 12 was not speaking about all of the laws of the Torah. In fact, at the time that this commandment was given, Israel had not even left Egypt, nor had God given the laws at Mount Sinai, nor had Moses descended the mountain with the tablets.

This verse simply explains that if the *ger* desired to participate in making a Passover-lamb sacrifice, he must follow the same procedure as the native-born Israelite. In the Hebrew Bible, the word *torah* has multiple meanings. In certain cases, the word is used to refer collectively to all of the laws in the Pentateuch. In other cases, it can denote only a subsection of laws or a single law. For example:

> Command Aaron and his sons, saying, This is the law [*torah*] of the burnt offering. The burnt offering shall be on the hearth on the altar all night until the morning, and the fire of the altar shall be kept burning on it. (Leviticus 6:9)

Exodus 12 uses the term *torah* in a similar sense. A parallel passage regarding the "second Passover" confirms this. A special Passover sacrifice may be offered in the second month in the event that it could not have been offered at its proper time:

> And if a stranger sojourns among you and would keep the Passover to the LORD, according to the statute of the Passover and according to its rule, so shall he do. You shall have one statute [*chukkah achat*, חקה אחת], both for the sojourner [*ger*] and for the native. (Numbers 9:14)

In this case, the same idea communicated by *torah* (law) in Exodus 12 is now described as a *chukkah* (statute), which does not ordinarily apply to the whole body of commandments. Thus, we can see that in Exodus, "one law" is Passover-specific. Jacob Milgrom underscores the idea of Passover being voluntary for the non-Israelite:

> The *ger* is under no obligation to observe the festivals. The paschal sacrifice is explicitly declared voluntary for the *ger:* whereas an Israelite abstains from the sacrifice on pain of *karet,* the *ger* may observe it provided he is circumcised.[44]

We find the same type of distinction when it comes to the commandment of building and dwelling in a *sukkah*. Leviticus 23:42 explicitly states that "all native Israelites" are required to dwell in the *sukkah*, thus implying that it is optional for the *ger*.[45]

Therefore, "one law" does not imply equal obligation. The *ger* can participate in a Passover sacrifice if he wants to, but the Israelite absolutely must do so. The *ger* could opt out of the Passover but would still be considered part of the broader community. The one *torah* that applies to both of them is the single law requiring both to be circumcised in order to eat the Passover sacrifice.

MORE ON ONE LAW

The language of "one law" appears again in several other contexts throughout the Torah dealing with the *ger*. Because its proper understanding is vital to how we view the non-Israelite obligation to the Torah, we will examine each occurrence.

> The guilt offering is just like the sin offering; there is one law [*torah achat*] for them. The priest who makes atonement with it shall have it. (Leviticus 7:7)

Here, the usage of the phrase "one law" precludes any possibility that the phrase means the Torah as a whole. Instead, we are to understand that the specific sacrificial procedures are the same in both cases.

Numbers 15 uses similar terminology. Once more, the context is the sacrificial service:

> And if a stranger is sojourning with you, or anyone is living permanently among you, and he wishes to offer a food offering, with a pleasing aroma to the LORD, he shall do as you do. For the assembly, there shall be one statute [*chukkah achat*] for you and for the stranger [*ger*] who sojourns with you, a statute forever throughout your generations. You and the sojourner [*ger*] shall be alike before the LORD. One law [*torah achat*] and one rule [*mishpat echad*, משפט אחד] shall be for you and for the stranger [*ger*] who sojourns with you. (Numbers 15:14–16)

> And the priest shall make atonement before the LORD for the person who makes a mistake, when he sins unintentionally, to make atonement for him, and he shall be forgiven. You shall have one law [*torah achat*] for him

who does anything unintentionally, for him who is native among the people of Israel and for the stranger [*ger*] who sojourns among them. (Numbers 15:28–29)

Here, the application is similar to previous cases. In the first passage, if the *ger* wishes to offer a sacrifice, he must do it in the Torah-prescribed manner just as the Israelite would. In the second passage, the same ritual procedure regarding a sin offering applies to both the *ger* and the native-born. The phrases "one statute" (*chukkah achat*) and "one rule" (*mishpat echad*) further substantiate that "one law" is meant in a specific way rather than referring to the body of Torah law as a whole.

When we read and apply the passages that speak of "one law" in their original context, it becomes apparent that they do not mean that the entire Torah should apply identically to both the Israelite and the *ger*. Milgrom takes this approach, noting that one must not make sweeping generalizations based on these verses:

> The injunction that "there shall be one law for you and the resident stranger" (Num. 15:15; cf. Exodus 12:48–49; Lev. 7:7; 24:22; Num. 9:14; 15:29–30) should not be misconstrued. It applies only to the case given in the context; it is not to be taken as a generalization.[46]

THE OBLIGATIONS OF THE GER

Here is one remaining example of "one-law" language, found in Leviticus 24:

> Whoever kills an animal shall make it good, and whoever kills a person shall be put to death. You shall have the same rule [*mishpat echad*] for the sojourner [*ger*] and for the native, for I am the LORD your God. (Leviticus 24:21–22)

Unlike all of the other "one-law" passages cited above, these verses are not in a sacrificial context. They do not actually speak of "one *torah*"; instead, they indicate that there must be "one judgment," referring to the judicial procedure and sentence to be meted out by the court for a crime. This stands in contrast to other judicial systems in the ancient Near East, where outsiders would not be given the same sentence, judicial process, rights, or legal protection as natives if they were victims or perpetrators of civil crimes.[47]

This passage implies equal rights for both the stranger and the native-born in the courts, and it demands equal responsibility for such acts as negligence and murder. This idea of equality before the law is reinforced in another passage where the non-Israelite is given equal access to the six cities of refuge:

> These six cities shall be for refuge for the people of Israel, and for the stranger [*ger*] and for the sojourner among them, that anyone who kills any person without intent may flee there. (Numbers 35:15)

If a *ger* had committed involuntary manslaughter he could flee to one of these cities for safety, but if he had committed the act with intent he must face the death penalty. Additionally, according to Leviticus 17:7–9, there was to be the same prohibition of and punishment for idolatry in regard to the non-Israelite as there was for the Israelite.

Even in some cases of ritual purity we find similar injunctions:

> And every person who eats what dies of itself or what is torn by beasts, whether he is a native or a sojourner [*ger*], shall wash his clothes and bathe himself in water and be unclean until the evening; then he shall be clean. But if he does not wash them or bathe his flesh, he shall bear his iniquity. (Leviticus 17:15–16)

Yet, we do find more distinctions. For example we read in the Ten Commandments that while the Israelite is specifically forbidden to work on Shabbat, the non-Israelite is not enjoined to rest on the Sabbath; it only says that he may not be forced to do work.[48]

The Sabbath commandment is given to the Israelites; the mention of the *ger* is completely secondary as a servant or non-Jew among the people of Israel. The non-Israelite participates in Shabbat but not on the same level as the Israelite; the obligations are different. In Deuteronomy 14:21, we find a specific distinction in relation to a dietary command. A *ger* may eat what an Israelite is explicitly forbidden to eat.[49]

Drawing specific conclusions as to the implications and ins-and-outs of exactly what this meant for the Torah-observant *ger* is difficult; nevertheless scholars have drawn some big-picture conclusions. Once again Jacob Milgrom weighs in:

> Though the *ger* enjoyed equal protection with the Israelite under the law, he was not of the same legal status; he neither enjoyed the same privileges nor was bound by the same obligations. Whereas the civil law held the citizen and the *ger* of equal status (e.g., Lev 24:22; Num 35:15), the religious law made distinctions according to the following underlining principle: The *ger* is bound by the prohibitive commandments but not by performative ones.[50]

Milgrom himself admits that his conclusions are a generalization; nevertheless some important general principles can be established.

OPPORTUNITY VERSUS OBLIGATION

One more key point must be mentioned in regard to the distinction between the *ger* and the Israelite. In the case of the priest and Levite and man and woman, etc., the distinctive commandments for each group are unique and should really not be performed by other groups. For example, a non-Israelite is certainly not encouraged to voluntarily take on the prohibitions and injunctions of the priest. In fact, to do so would at times cause him actually to transgress the Torah rather than to fulfill additional commandments, and the same is the case with men and women.

Yet, this is not necessarily true of the non-Israelite observing Israelite-specific instructions. In the case of Passover, as we saw, although not obligated to do so, a *ger* may choose to participate in the Passover sacrifice, provided that he does it in the prescribed manner, which includes circumcision. Biblical scholar Patrick Miller comments:

> The resident alien, for the most part, was not excluded from participation in the ritual practices of Israel's cultic life, specifically the festivals and cults of Israel ... The

resident alien was not required but was permitted to participate in those actions that involved the active worship of [the Lord].[51]

The *ger* was not obligated to do so, but he had the opportunity to join in with native-born in their festivals and various other Torah rituals as worship unto the God of Israel. Therefore, unlike with the distinctions between Israelite and priest and man and woman, the non-Jew had opportunity to take on more than what was required of him.

KEEP THE COMMANDMENTS

It would be wrong to take the model of the *ger* and try to apply it directly to all Gentile believers in Messiah today. There are many more factors to figure in, such as how the apostles themselves would have interpreted the word *ger*, the rulings they made such as in Acts 15, and the fact that most Gentile believers today are not living in the land of Israel or in the midst of a Jewish community. Instead, the purpose of the present chapter is merely to demonstrate that there are indeed biblical distinctions within the Torah as to the commandment-obligations of Jews and Gentiles.

With this understanding we can better understand apostolic passages such as, "For this is the love of God, that we keep his commandments" (1 John 5:3), and "Neither circumcision counts for anything nor uncircumcision, but keeping the commandments of God" (1 Corinthians 7:19). These passages were written to communities that contained both Jews and Gentiles. Each person hearing these words would have understood "commandments" as referring to the specific parts of Torah that applied to them as a Jew or Gentile and man or woman.

In the 1 Corinthians passage, Paul states that the uncircumcised Gentile believer should keep the commandments that apply to him and that the circumcised Jewish believer should keep the commandments that apply to him.

> Paul can only mean that Gentiles should obey commandments also, although evidently not the same ones as Jews. He views Gentiles as included in the perspective of the

Creator which involves commandments for all ... The saying would then imply that whether or not one is a Jew does not matter before God, but whether one performs the commandments incumbent upon one does.[52]

In Messiah everyone is in equal standing before God as regards salvation, but we all have our individual responsibilities. There is only one Torah for all of God's people, but within that one Torah are many different distinctions. Once we understand that the Torah itself makes these distinctions, it becomes easier for us to grasp the words of the apostles because, after all, it is the Torah from which they themselves are drawing.

So far, we have identified that the New Testament speaks of two different types of believers: Jews and Gentiles. We have learned that the laws of the Torah applied differently to Jews and Gentiles. This lays the groundwork for introducing the Apostolic-Era Gentile believers—the people to whom Paul addressed most of his letters: the God-fearers.

CHAPTER THREE

THE GOD-FEARERS

> So Peter opened his mouth and said, "Truly I understand
> that God shows no partiality, but in every nation anyone
> who fears him and does what is right is acceptable to
> him." (Acts 10:34–35)

By examining the distinctions that exist between Jews and Gentiles within the Torah of Moses we are now ready to approach the situations of Gentiles in the midst of Judaism in the late Second-Temple period. By the first century CE, Israel's religious life was in full swing. The remodeled Temple in Jerusalem shone in all its glory, and the Jewish people thrived, both in their homeland and abroad in the Diaspora. Despite Judea's issues with the Roman government, Judaism of the late Second-Temple Period attracted many Gentiles who wished to join themselves to the God of Abraham, Isaac, and Jacob. The Torah's ethical monotheism influenced Gentiles in Judea as well as in much of the Diaspora, where Judaism became increasingly in vogue. Many Gentiles chose to go through full ritual conversion to Judaism, yet many more wished to take on monotheism in association with the Jewish people without becoming full proselytes. Those who underwent full conversion attained a legal status as Jews. Those who did not become full proselytes still worshipped and fellowshipped with the Jewish community, but they did not enjoy Jewish status, privilege, or responsibility.[53]

First-century Judaism referred to this latter type of semi-converted Gentiles as "God-fearers" (*yir'ei HaShem*, ירֵאי יי, or *yir'ei shamayim*, ירֵאי שמים). While not a technical term per se, it referred to "non-Jews who adopted certain Jewish practices without actually converting to Judaism."[54] In essence it was "an umbrella term for Gentiles with varied interests in Judaism."[55] The Jewish community expected these God-fearers to hold themselves to the moral, Noachide laws of the Torah, but many observed additional commandments of Torah on different levels. For example, to various extents, God-fearers kept the Sabbath, the festivals, and the dietary laws. Some even underwent circumcision, particularly in the second generation.[56] Through their observance of the Torah they expressed their love for the God of Israel.

Some scholars estimate that millions of Gentiles became God-fearers in the first-century Roman world. This group of people can give us a window into the earliest Gentile followers of Yeshua.

THE PSALMS

The Psalms introduce the concept of the God-fearer as a non-Jew worshipping among Israel. Several passages from the Psalms divide God's people into three categories: Israel, the house of Aaron, and "those who fear the LORD" (*yir'ei HaShem*).

1. Let *Israel* say, "His steadfast love endures forever."
2. Let *the house of Aaron* say, "His steadfast love endures forever."
3. Let *those who fear the LORD* say, "His steadfast love endures forever." (Psalm 118:2–4)

1. O *Israel*, trust in the LORD! He is their help and their shield.
2. O *house of Aaron*, trust in the LORD! He is their help and their shield.
3. You *who fear the LORD*, trust in the LORD! He is their help and their shield. (Psalm 115:9–11)

1. He will bless *the house of Israel*;
2. He will bless *the house of Aaron*;
3. He will bless *those who fear the LORD*, both the small and the great. (Psalm 115:12–13)

Some Psalms contain the additional category of the house of Levi:

1. O house of Israel, bless the LORD!
2a. O *house of Aaron*, bless the LORD!
2b. O *house of Levi*, bless the LORD!
3. You *who fear the LORD*, bless the LORD! (Psalm 135:19–20)

The last category, "those who fear the LORD," implies Gentiles worshipping in the midst of the people of Israel who had joined themselves to the Jewish people yet retained their identity as being from the nations.[57] In that regard, the first-century God-fearer phenomena has its roots all the way back in the First-Temple period.

ANCIENT EVIDENCE

Writings from the first five centuries CE provide a plethora of literary evidence for the existence of the God-fearers as a recognizable class within Judaism.[58] They are mentioned by name in rabbinic literature.[59] For example, in the midrash we read that in the days of Messiah, the people of Israel will identify themselves as members of the nation belonging to the LORD. One will say "I am the LORD's"; another will "call on the name of Jacob"; another will inscribe a sign on his hand saying, "Belonging to the LORD"; and another will "name Israel's name." The sages saw these as four types of people who comprise the eschatological people of God: the righteous, the proselyte, the penitent, and the God-fearer.

> Four types of pious ones stand before the Almighty; as it says [in Isaiah 44:5], "One will say, 'I am the LORD's.'" This nation will say, "I am the LORD's." He belongs completely to the Almighty, and has no sinful ways in him. "One will call on the name of Jacob." This refers to the righteous proselyte [i.e., convert]. "Another shall write on his hand, 'Belonging to the LORD.'" This refers to the penitents. One "will name Israel's name with honor." This refers to the God-fearers [Gentiles]. (*Numbers Rabbah* 8:2)

According to the midrash, the fourth category of "pious ones" is the God-fearers. They are Gentiles who have repudiated idolatry and attached themselves to the God of Israel. They "name Israel's name with honor," a phrase better translated as "name himself by the name of Israel" (Isaiah 44:5). They are not legally named Israel by the Jewish authorities, but they voluntarily adopt identity within the people without undergoing legal conversion.

Several other examples could be cited. The sages referred to both the Gentile King Lemuel's father (from the book of Proverbs) and a senator of the Roman emperor as God-fearers.[60] In another passage in the midrash, the sages ask what merit spares the wicked coastal cities like Antioch, Gaza, and Ashkelon from total destruction. The rabbis believed that HaShem spares such cities from annihilation for the sake of the righteous Gentile God-fearers therein.

> Yet for whose sake do they stand? For the sake of one nation and one God-fearing person whom the Holy One, blessed be He, receives from their hands. (*Genesis Rabbah* 28:5)

The God-fearers even made secular histories. The historian Josephus speaks of "a great many of the Greeks" who are attracted to Judaism in Antioch and in turn join in with Israel.[61] Epictetus the philosopher (first century CE) asks the question of certain Gentiles: "Why do you act the part of a Jew when you are a Greek?"[62] He is referring to the God-fearers who are not fully recognized as Jews yet behave and worship like them. Juvenal the Roman poet speaks scathingly of Gentiles who take on Jewish practices:

> Some who have had a father who reveres the Sabbath, worship nothing but the clouds, and the divinity of the heavens, and see no difference between eating swine's flesh, from which their father abstained, and that of man; and in time they take to circumcision. Having been wont to flout the laws of Rome, they learn and practice and revere the Jewish law, and all that Moses committed to his secret tome, forbidding to point out the way to any not worshipping the same rites, and conducting none but the circumcised to the desired fountain. For all which the father was to blame, who gave up every seventh day

to idleness, keeping it apart from all the concerns of life. (Juvenal, *Satires* 14)[63]

His description matches perfectly that of the God-fearing Gentile.

God-fearers even appear in ancient inscriptions. For example, a third-century CE inscription found in the Greek city of Aphrodisias contained a list of individuals who had contributed financially to a Jewish community building. The list included both Jews and a separate category of God-fearers (*theosebeis*, θεοσεβεις). Louis Feldman writes:

> The *theosebeis* not only donate to a Jewish community charity, two of them are members of the Jewish association for, among other things, study and prayer, referred to in the introduction of the inscription. It is clear that the *theosebeis* are gentiles interested in the Jewish religion, and attached, however loosely, to the Jewish community. The word *theosebeis* is just another version of the "God-fearer." If that is true at Aphrodisias, it is probably true elsewhere, where *theosebeis* also contributed to Jewish causes … Some God-fearers in Aphrodisias studied the law; many elsewhere observed the Sabbath rest and other customs. The extent to which they obeyed Jewish law seems to have been up to the God-fearers themselves.[64]

This inscription is evidence of the existence of God-fearers not only in Aphrodisias but in other locations as well. Based on this archeological find, Shlomo Pines speculates that "groups of 'God-fearers' were to be found in many countries within the Roman Empire and also beyond its frontiers."[65] As we shall see, the ubiquitous presence of the God-fearers throughout the Diaspora provided the perfect foundation for the spread of the gospel among the non-Jewish nations.

THE NEW TESTAMENT

Turning to the New Testament, in passages such as John 12:20, we find evidence of Gentiles worshipping among Jews. Some speculate that Paul refers to God-fearers in Romans 2:14: "For when Gentiles, who do not have the law, by nature do what the law requires, they are a law to themselves, even though they do not have the law." Although the Gentile God-fearers have not been given the Torah in the same manner as the Jews (i.e., they do not have the law), they nevertheless choose to obey it.

The book of Acts contains several clear references to God-fearers. They are referred to by the terms *foboumenoi* ("those fearing," φοβουμενοι) and *sebomenoi ton theon* ("those reverencing God," σεβομενοι τον θεον). The first instance occurs in Acts 10:

> At Caesarea there was a man named Cornelius, a centurion of what was known as the Italian Cohort, a devout man *who feared God* with all his household, gave alms generously to the people, and prayed continually to God … And they said, "Cornelius, a centurion, an upright and *God-fearing man*, who is well spoken of by the whole Jewish nation." (Acts 10:1–2, 22; my emphasis)

Cornelius is referred to as a "man who fears God." Reading on, we see that he is "devout," gives alms, and prays at the liturgical times of prayer, which results in his being spoken well of by the Jewish people. No doubt this is only a small sampling of the Torah practices that Cornelius had chosen to take upon himself.[66] The language here suggests that, while he had not attained legal Jewish status, he was closely connected with the people of Israel.

Paul addressed the crowd in Acts 13:26 as "men of Israel and you who fear God," indicating that he spoke to both Jews and righteous Gentiles. The title "devout women" and the description of Lydia and Titius Justus as "worshipper[s] of God" have the same connotation as God-fearers.[67]

The book of Acts (and other literary evidence) makes it clear that the spread of the gospel to non-Jews began first with the God-fearers. Pines write:

> The early Christian community was addressed chiefly, and perhaps solely, to these 'God-fearers', and that it had its first successes amongst them.[68]

Because the God-fearing Gentiles were already oriented toward Israel and Judaism, the apostles found them to be the perfect soil in which to begin planting the seeds of Yeshua's message. Unlike the pagan world around them, the God-fearers had already accepted Jewish monotheism. They were familiar with the Torah and the Prophets, attended synagogue, and functioned within Jewish communities. It was but a small step for them to understand that salvation had come to the world through the Jewish Messiah. Pines points to further clues of the early impact of the gospel upon God-fearers:

> In Pahlavi, Sogdian, and New Persian, the meaning of one of the most popular designations for Christians is 'fearers'… The designation of the Christians by the name tarsākān [fearers] is, consequently, further proof of the strong connections which existed in the Iranian regions (and in the Eastern border-lands of the Roman Empire) between Christianity and of the [God-fearers].[69]

Today, in certain parts of the Middle East, Christians are still known as "fearers," a vestige from the earliest days of Christianity when Gentile believers in Messiah were made up largely of God-fearers.

David Flusser believed it is this God-fearing status that the Jerusalem Council grants to the new Gentile converts in Messiah.[70] Acts 15 looses Gentile believers from the expectation that they undergo legal conversion and take on the full weight of the Torah, and instead imposes upon them four essentials. As with the God-fearers' minimal adherence to the moral code of the Torah, the four stipulations served only as a starting point for Gentiles. The rest of the Torah and Scriptures remained open before them. Flusser states:

> The Noachide precepts were only seen as the minimal condition for Gentiles to be recognized as God-fearers. They were so understood by the God-fearers themselves, who were attracted by the Jewish way of life and accepted many Jewish commandments without becoming full proselytes. This was the attitude of many Christian God-fearers … many of which wished to observe as many Jewish precepts as they could. It is evident that, while the leadership of the Mother Church decided to lay no

burden upon the Gentile believers beyond the Noachide precepts (Acts 15:28–29; see Gal. 2:6), it did not object to their voluntarily observing more.[71]

While many Gentiles would be eager to take on as much Torah as they could, the apostles ruled against obligating the new Gentile believers to the entire yoke of the Torah. As God-fearers, the Gentiles were able to join in with Israel and participate on a level that still allowed them interaction with their fellow non-believing Gentile friends and relatives.

SPIRITUAL PROSELYTES

Today, many Gentile believers in Messiah are returning to the Jewish roots of Christianity and the practice of Torah. We are resurrecting the *yir'ei HaShem*, the God-fearers of old. Some scholars today refer to God-fearers as "spiritual converts." That label seems to fit perfectly into the Pauline language about one who is "a Jew is one inwardly" where "circumcision is a matter of the heart."[72] The ancient God-fearers were Gentiles who did not become legally Jewish but instead had a strong connection to and respect for the Jewish people, so much so that they even took upon themselves an identity within the religion of Israel. The believing God-fearer today does the same through Messiah Yeshua, the Messiah of Israel.

Although believing Gentiles in Messiah have a greater standing in the kingdom of God than the first-century God-fearer outside of Messiah, the title God-fearer is very apropos. God-fearers were not compelled to keep the Jewish aspects of Torah such as circumcision or Sabbath by decree or law. They did so out of a sincere and intense love for God's Torah and his ways. They saw the light of Israel and sought to draw themselves close to it, so that they might warm themselves in its glow. As Gentile believers today realize that Messiah has spiritually grafted them into the nation of Israel, they feel drawn to the Jewish people and desire to worship alongside God's chosen as fellow-heirs of the covenants and promises. Just like the God-fearers of old, we too have cast our lot with Israel.

But the questions still remain: How much Torah is required of a God-fearing believer? Which laws of the Torah apply to God-fearing Gentile believers?

CHAPTER FOUR

THE GENTILE BELIEVER'S
TORAH OBLIGATION

> For you know how, like a father with his children, we exhorted each one of you and encouraged you and charged you to walk in a manner worthy of God, who calls you into his own kingdom and glory. (1 Thessalonians 2:11–12)

A s we have seen, the Torah and the rest of the Scriptures preserve a healthy distinction between Jews and righteous Gentiles and differentiate between their respective relationships to the commandments of the Torah. Jewish believers have the responsibility of ongoing covenantal fidelity to the Torah that began when Israel accepted the full yoke of the Torah at Mount Sinai.[73] For Gentile disciples, things are a bit more complicated; while non-Jewish believers are not obligated in the same way as Jewish believers, they too have certain biblical responsibilities towards a Torah life.

In his book on Galatians, D. Thomas Lancaster articulates that the apostles did not bind the Torah's "sign commandments" and distinctive identity markers upon the Gentile believers. These are the commandments specifically given to Israel as marks of distinction such as Shabbat, tzitzit, and circumcision—the last of which figures most predominately in Paul's letters. While Gentiles are not forbidden to participate in these commandments of Jewish identity, they are not bound to keep them as Jews are. (Note: We will talk more about these "sign commandments" in the coming chapters.)

At the same time, believers sometimes assume that HaShem's Torah applies only to Jews and not to Gentile disciples at all. Nothing could be further from the truth. Despite the fact that the apostles "loosed" the Gentiles from these sign commandments, for the most part they are bound to the rest of the Torah's commandments. It should be emphasized that Gentiles in Messiah have a status in the people of God and a responsibility to Torah that far exceeds that of the God-fearer of the ancient synagogue and that of the modern-day Noachide (Son of Noah). Through Yeshua, believing Gentiles have been grafted in to the people of God and become members of the commonwealth of Israel. While membership has its privileges, it also has its obligations.

ACTS 15: THE FOUR PROHIBITIONS

It would be best to begin a discussion about a Gentile believer's obligation to the Torah right where the apostles did, with the ruling of the Jerusalem Council. After much debate, the apostles declared that the Gentile disciples do not need to convert to Judaism and thus should not be bound to the full yoke of the Torah. As we learned in chapter one, God had already shown his approval of Gentiles in Messiah by giving them the Spirit before circumcision. Instead, these new converts should, at a minimum, observe four essential prohibitions:

> Therefore my judgment is that we should not trouble those of the Gentiles who turn to God, but should write to them to abstain from the things polluted by idols, and from sexual immorality, and from what has been strangled, and from blood. For from ancient generations Moses has had in every city those who proclaim him, for he is read every Sabbath in the synagogues. (Acts 15:19–21) [74]

They were instructed to abstain from: things contaminated by idols, sexual immorality, from what has been strangled, and from blood. At first glance it appears that the Gentiles have very few commandments to deal with, but upon closer examination each of these four prohibitions becomes, in a sense, an overarching category which contains many sub-category commandments.

This may be one of the reasons the Apostle James adds the phrase about Moses being read in the synagogue every Sabbath. The new Gentile believer would need to attend the local synagogue to learn how each of these four prohibitions plays out practically in everyday life. Let's take a closer look at these four essential prohibitions.

THINGS CONTAMINATED BY IDOLS

Although there is no explicit *mitzvah* in the Torah to refrain from food sacrificed to idols, rabbinically this is derived from Deuteronomy 7:26:

> And you shall not bring an abominable thing into your house and become devoted to destruction like it. You shall utterly detest and abhor it, for it is devoted to destruction.

The Torah stipulates that the Israelite was not to derive any benefit whatsoever from idols, objects of *avodah zarah* ("foreign worship," עבודה זרה), or from anything that has been offered up to an idol. This becomes especially applicable to food which, in the pagan world, was often sacrificed to idols, and thus this became a major issue in the time of the apostles. In another pertinent passage, the Torah forbids Jews to "whore after their gods," "sacrifice to their gods," or "eat of his sacrifice," that is, food sacrificed to idols.[75] The apostles extended this prohibition to Gentile believers. The prohibition is, therefore, binding on them as well.

Eating food contaminated by idols is such an important prohibition that it is brought up again in the book of Revelation.[76] This prohibition also appears in early church literature such as the *Didache* and Justin Martyr's *Dialogue with Trypho the Jew,* and by no less influential teachers in the early church than Clement of Alexandria, Irenaeus, Tertullian, and the forth- through fifth-century church father Augustine.[77]

While Acts 15 only deals with food sacrificed to idols, the apostles surely meant this to also include all forms of idolatry. It is in this spirit that Paul gives the injunction to "flee from idolatry" (1 Corinthians 10:14). The New Testament writers frequently admonish the new Gentile believers to refrain from *avodah zarah* and remind them that idolatry is part of their pre-Messiah life—something to be left behind.[78] New Testament scholar Paul Barnett writes:

> Paul's call to turn from idols was fundamental to his proclamation of the gospel. To return to idolatry, or to fail to disengage from it, would be to receive the grace of God in vain.[79]

It is important to note for our discussion that this is not "an ethical demand so much as a *ritual* command."[80] Paul and the apostles drew upon the quintessential injunction against idolatry found in the Ten Commandments. After HaShem identifies himself as the one who brought Israel out of Egypt, he makes it clear that to follow him means rejection of all other gods:

> You shall have no other gods before me. You shall not make for yourself a carved image, or any likeness of anything that is in heaven above, or that is in the earth beneath, or that is in the water under the earth. You shall not bow down to them or serve them. (Exodus 20:3–5)

Both the worship and creation of graven images was forbidden. It appears that the early assembly of Messiah shared Judaism's strict aversion to three-dimensional images, even if the images were not intended for worship. Origen writes that such art "attracts the attention of foolish men."[81] In fact, "up until the second century neither literary nor archaeological sources give any evidence of Christian art."[82] But this second of the Ten Commandments is really just a subheading for numerous other commandments throughout the Torah that forbid both the participation in *avodah zarah* as well as imitating any of the practices of pagan religions.

> You shall not do as they do in the land of Egypt, where you lived, and you shall not do as they do in the land of Canaan, to which I am bringing you. You shall not walk in their statutes. (Leviticus 18:3)

Over forty-five of the 613 commandments in the Torah deal exclusively with forbidding *avodah zarah* and what to do with those who practice *avodah zarah*. It therefore goes without saying that the apostles would have viewed all of these commandments as fully binding on the Gentile converts coming into the community. They considered it imperative that the new believers make a clean break from their idolatrous past and cling to the God of Israel. Therefore, all the Torah's commandments regarding idolatry are binding on Gentile disciples.

SEXUAL IMMORALITY

Next is the injunction to abstain from sexual immorality (*gillui arayot*, גלוי עריות). Once again this is not an end to itself but rather a general injunction. We find the details throughout the Torah in the over twenty-five commandments dealing with proper sexual relations. This prohibition of Acts 15 is likely based upon Leviticus chapters 18 and 20 where a plethora of commandants regarding sexual relations are given. Here's a sampling:

> And you shall not take a woman as a rival wife to her sister, uncovering her nakedness while her sister is still alive. You shall not approach a woman to uncover her nakedness while she is in her menstrual uncleanness. And you shall not lie sexually with your neighbor's wife and so make yourself unclean with her. You shall not lie with a male as with a woman; it is an abomination. And you shall not lie with any animal and so make yourself unclean with it, neither shall any woman give herself to an animal to lie with it: it is perversion. (Leviticus 18:18–23)

If the Gentiles were commanded to abstain from sexual practices that are immoral, it would therefore make sense that they would need to learn what practices are forbidden. According to these two chapters of Leviticus, improper relations include bestiality, homosexuality, and incest. While most conservative Christians and Messianic believers today assume those prohibitions are universal, one sexual prohibition frequently overlooked is that of relations with a woman during her monthly cycle. In Hebrew, this period of time is called *niddah* (נדה) meaning "impurity," which the rabbis have interpreted to imply "separation." Leviticus 15 gives further details regarding this injunction including the length of time for this period of separation.[83]

Additionally, based on Leviticus 18:6, which states, "None of you shall approach any one of his close relatives to uncover nakedness," Judaism enforces certain safeguards that prevent even hints or appearances of sexual immorality. The Hebrew word translated "nakedness" is *ervah* (ערוה) and actually has a much wider connotation of immodest behavior in general. The sages reason: If one should be this careful with one's "blood relative" (i.e., one's family), how much more so with non-relatives. Practices such as *shmirat negi'ah* ("guarding touch," שמירת נגיעה), which limits even casual physical touch between a man and woman who are neither married nor related; *issur yichud* ("prohibition of seclusion," איסור יחוד), where an unmarried man and woman would take care not to be secluded alone in a private place; and *tzeni'ut* ("modesty," צניעות),[84] the praxis of men and women dressing and acting modestly all help to guard against even the appearance of evil (1 Thessalonians 5:22)[85]—not to mention the Torah's commandment prohibiting cross-dressing (Deuteronomy 22:5). All of these issues fall within the category of sexual purity.

Also included would be the injunction of marriage through a proper ceremony, which the sages derive from the verse "When a man takes a wife and marries her" (Deuteronomy 24:1). This includes both the betrothal period (*kiddushin*, קדושין) and the marriage (*nissu'in*, נשואין). The prohibitions of improper sexual relations only make sense if the institution of marriage exists through a proper Torah-ordained ceremony. Paul makes several references to the institution of marriage in his various letters to Gentile congregations.[86] Along with that comes the Torah's prohibition on adultery, and the Torah's prohibitions on promiscuity, prostitution, and sexual relationships outside of marriage. Sex out of wedlock, prostitution, and promiscuity all fall under the single Hebrew word *zenut* (זנות), ordinarily translated into English as "harlotry" or "whoredom." The Torah's use of the word is not limited to acts of sex-for-hire; it includes any and all extramarital sexual contact.[87]

All in all, rather than one simple injunction, refraining from sexual immorality is an umbrella mitzvah that includes dozens of further detailed commandments from the Torah. The Torah's commandments prohibiting sexual immorality are binding upon Gentile believers.

THINGS STRANGLED AND BLOOD

Let's continue our examination of the four essential prohibitions of Acts 15. Although we have two left, they deal with different aspects of the same issue. The first is to abstain "from what is strangled [*pniktos*, πνικτος]." The majority of Bible scholars see this language as a prohibition against eating meat that has not been ritually slaughtered according to Jewish standards. Here are a few examples:

> "Strangled meat" referred to animals that had been slaughtered in a manner that left the blood in it. Blood was considered sacred to Jews, and all meat was to be drained of blood before consuming it.[88]

> "What has been strangled," i.e., meat from animals improperly or not ritually butchered, without having the blood drained from them (Leviticus 17:15 cf. 7:24; Exodus 22:31).[89]

> "Strangled meat" i.e., meat from animals not slaughtered by pouring out their blood, in conformity with biblical and Jewish practice.[90]

Meat that has been "strangled" refers to meat that has been improperly slaughtered, i.e., not by the traditional method of Jewish slaughter (*shechitah*, שחיטה). Some interpreters have been confused by the negative proscription, but this is just the "negative corollary" to the positive commandment in Leviticus 17:13 to "pour out the blood."[91] We see an example of this usage of "strangled" in the Mishnah where a method of improper slaughter using a dull instrument is called one that "strangulates".[92] Strangled is also used this way in the writings of Philo and the apocryphal work *Joseph and Aseneth*.[93] When interpreted in the Jewish framework within which the injunction was given, "things strangled" is directly related to the prohibitions against "blood."

> The prohibition of "blood" came under the same requirement, referring to the consumption of the blood of animals in any form. These three requirements [abstention from food sacrificed to idols, things strangled, and blood]

were thus all ritual, dealing with matters of clean and unclean food.[94]

The fourth prohibition of blood is connected to the prohibition of strangulation. Without proper slaughter the blood remains in the meat.

The Jewish method of slaughter by *shechitah* is very ancient, derived from sacrificial procedure of the holy priesthood, and designed to remove as much blood as possible. It involves the precise slitting of the throat among other regulations. The sages insist that it goes all the way back to Mount Sinai. They find an allusion to this in Deuteronomy 12:21 (NASB): "You may slaughter ... as I have commanded you." To the sages this meant that God showed Moses and the children of Israel the correct way to slaughter the meat as is implied in the phrase "as I commanded you." Although the precise method of slaughter is not recorded in the text, it was passed down orally. Hebrew scholar Jeffery Tigay sees further linguistic support for the traditional position:

> This clause implies a prescribed method of slaughter. The text's use of the verb *zavach*, which refers to sacrificial slaughter, indicates that secular slaughter is to be performed by the method used in sacrificial slaughter, namely slitting the animal's throat.[95]

Because the Hebrew word *zavach* (זבח) is used in a technical sense in other places regarding the manner of slaughter of sacrificial animals, it implies that the same procedure is to be employed for non-Temple slaughter.

Church history scholar Oskar Skarsaune finds evidence in early church literature of Gentile believers in France still purchasing kosher-slaughtered meat even after the church had begun severing its ties from Judaism:

> There is an interesting hint in the narrative itself. Under torture, a girl named Biblias in a sudden burst of indignation said, "How can those eat children, who are forbidden to eat the blood even of brute beasts?" This clearly indicates that the community of Lyons [France] still observed the apostolic decree of Acts 15 concerning kosher meat.

As Frend aptly remarks, "The question arises, where did the Christians get their meat from? The only possible answer is from a kosher market established for the Jews and Christians in the City."[96]

Therefore, as late as the end of the second century there were still Gentile Christians who observed the strict prohibition against blood consumption and only ate kosher-slaughtered meat.

Yet, just as with the prohibitions of food sacrificed to idols and sexual immorality, it may be that the apostles intended the prohibition categorically. It may imply more of the Torah's dietary commandants. For one thing, it would have forced the Gentile disciples to acquire only kosher-slaughtered meat. If they were purchasing meat only from Jewish slaughterers, they would be avoiding unkosher mammals such as swine and camel by default.[97] It seems on a subtle level that the apostles were pushing Gentiles towards a basic kosher diet. After all, as we pointed out, many of the new Gentile believers, such as Cornelius, were God-fearers and would have been keeping a kosher diet on some level as well.[98]

We find evidence of Apostolic-Era voices encouraging Gentiles towards a more kosher diet in an early Jewish-Christian document called the *Didache*. Written in the late first to early second century, it purports to contain instructions from the twelve apostles to the nations. We find some instructions regarding *kashrut*:

> If you can carry the whole yoke of the Lord, you will be perfect; but if you cannot, then do what you can. Concerning food, bear what you can, but carefully keep away from food sacrificed to idols, for it is a worship-service to gods from the realm of the dead. (*Didache* 6:2–3)

"Yoke of the Lord" here refers to the Torah. The *Didache* is calling for Gentiles "to do their best to eat food that is kosher—at the very least avoid eating meat that had been offered to idols."[99] Eating kosher was seen as the ideal, but room was made for those who would be unable to bear that yoke. In any case, at a minimum, Gentile disciples are obligated to keep the Torah's prohibitions on consuming blood and the meat of animals that have not been properly slaughtered.[100]

MURDER? THEFT? COVETING?

Some believers assume that the four essential prohibitions of Acts 15 are the only commandments incumbent on Gentile believers. What about obvious commandments such as the prohibitions on murder and theft? Are Gentiles exempt from these? Certainly not. Paul speaks of a few of these to the Gentile believers in Rome:

> For the commandments, "You shall not commit adultery, You shall not murder, You shall not steal, You shall not covet," and any other commandment, are summed up in this word: "You shall love your neighbor as yourself." Love does no wrong to a neighbor; therefore love is the fulfilling of the law. (Romans 13:9–10)

The apostles did not include in their list of obligations for Gentiles what Lancaster calls the "duh ... obvious" commandments.[101] Paul refers to the things in the Torah that are self-evident:

> Now the works of the flesh are evident: sexual immorality, impurity, sensuality, idolatry, sorcery, enmity, strife, jealousy, fits of anger, rivalries, dissensions, divisions, envy, drunkenness, orgies, and things like these. (Galatians 5:19–21)

The sages of Israel had a similar approach:

> The Torah states in Leviticus 18:4, "You shall fulfill my judgments." This refers to matters that, even if they had not been written down in the Torah, common sense would dictate that they should be written. They are idolatry, adultery, murder, robbery, and blasphemy." (b.*Yoma* 67b)

As with the four essentials of Acts 15, each of these injunctions needs to be understood categorically. They break down into further commandments. For example, the prohibition on murder includes not accepting a ransom for a murderer (Numbers 35:31), not standing by idly while someone's life is in danger (Leviticus 19:16), and the commandments surrounding the cities of refuge (e.g., Numbers 35:25). The prohibition of theft would include returning lost items back to their owner (Exodus 23:4), properly dealing with debt (e.g., Leviticus 19:13), and not having in one's possession unequal weights and measures (Deuteronomy 25:13).

Paul mentions the mitzvah of *kibbud av ve'em* ("honor father and mother," כבוד אב ואם) in his letter to the Ephesians:

> Children, obey your parents in the Lord, for this is right. "Honor your father and mother" (this is the first commandment with a promise), "that it may go well with you and that you may live long in the land." (Ephesians 6:1–3)[102]

The citation of this mitzvah is important, because many halachic authorities in the rabbinic world do not see this mitzvah as incumbent upon Gentiles.[103] Paul and the apostles did see it as binding on Gentile believers. Peter further elaborates by exhorting his readers to honor those in authority (1 Peter 2:17), which corresponds to the rabbinic interpretation of Leviticus 19:32: "Honor the face of an old man."[104]

From the Apostolic Scriptures, we can further ascertain that the apostles held Gentiles liable to the negative commandments against gossip (*lashon ha-ra*, לשון הרע),[105] and blasphemy (*chillul HaShem*, חלול השם),[106] and in the positive commandments of charity (*tzedakah*, צדקה),[107] Torah study (*talmud torah*, תלמוד תורה),[108] clinging to God (*devekut*, דבקות),[109] and hospitality (*hachnasat orchim*, הכנסת אורחים).[110]

We even find allusions to some of the commonsense commandments in Paul's midrashic use of the commandments. For example:

> Let the elders who rule well be considered worthy of double honor, especially those who labor in preaching and teaching. For the Scripture says, "You shall not muzzle an ox when it treads out the grain," and, "The laborer deserves his wages." (1 Timothy 5:17–18)[111]

Here Paul quotes the mitzvah of Deuteronomy 25:4 about not muzzling an ox. Although he uses it in an allegorical sense, the allegorical application can only be applied if the believers of Timothy's community hold the commandment to be binding in the literal sense as well. The injunction itself fits into the broader prohibition

against cruelty to animals (*tza'ar ba'alei chayim,* צער בעלי חיים)
which includes other injunctions such as not plowing a field with
two different kinds of animals (Deuteronomy 22:10) and shooing
the mother bird away before taking her eggs (Deuteronomy 22:6–7).

LOVE YOUR NEIGHBOR

There are some commandments that we would think of as "duh
… obvious" but which seem to specifically apply to the Jewish
nation and not to Gentiles. For example, Jewish tradition states that
the mitzvah to "love your neighbor as yourself" (Leviticus 19:18)
apparently refers only to one's fellow Jew. Yet the Master himself
challenged this interpretation when he expanded the meaning
of "neighbor" to extend to anyone who is in need.[112] Paul enjoins
this mitzvah on Gentile believers in Romans 13:9 and Galatians
5:14. Like the Master, Paul states that the commandment of love
categorically summarizes the other commandments of the Torah:
"For the whole [Torah] is fulfilled in one word: 'You shall love your
neighbor as yourself'" (Galatians 5:14). The "love-your-neighbor"
category finds expression in the numerous apostolic references
to "one another." For example:

> Love one another with brotherly affection. Outdo one
> another in showing honor. (Romans 12:10)
>
> Live in harmony with one another. (Romans 12:16)
>
> Owe no one anything, except to love each other. (Romans
> 13:8)
>
> Let us not pass judgment on one another any longer, but
> rather decide never to put a stumbling block or hindrance
> in the way of a brother. (Romans 14:13)
>
> Welcome one another as Christ has welcomed you.
> (Romans 15:7)
>
> When you come together to eat, wait for one another.
> (1 Corinthians 11:33)
>
> Through love serve one another. (Galatians 5:13)

Let us not become conceited, provoking one another, envying one another. (Galatians 5:26)

Walk in a manner worthy of the calling to which you have been called, with all humility and gentleness, with patience, bearing with one another in love. (Ephesians 4:1–2)

Be kind to one another, tenderhearted, forgiving one another. (Ephesians 4:32)

Do not lie to one another, seeing that you have put off the old self with its practices. (Colossians 3:9)

See that no one repays anyone evil for evil, but always seek to do good to one another and to everyone. (1 Thessalonians 5:15)

Love one another earnestly from a pure heart. (1 Peter 1:22)

Show hospitality to one another without grumbling. As each has received a gift, use it to serve one another. (1 Peter 4:9–10)

Not as though I were writing you a new commandment, but the one we have had from the beginning—that we love one another. And this is love, that we walk according to his commandments; this is the commandment, just as you have heard from the beginning, so that you should walk in it. (2 John 1:5–6)

These examples demonstrate that the commandment to "love your neighbor" is very broad, including all the other commandments falling into the category of neighbors and/or brothers. Commandments pertaining to "your brother" and "your neighbor" and "one another" should be interpreted in like manner, i.e., incumbent upon both Jews and Gentile believers in treating both Jews and Gentile believers.

Take for example the prohibition of not charging interest to your brother:

Take no interest from him or profit, but fear your God, that your brother may live beside you. You shall not lend him your money at interest, nor give him your food for profit. (Leviticus 25:36–37)

While this mitzvah is not specifically addressed in any of the New Testament, it falls into the "love-your-neighbor" category. The early Christian church, even after it had severed its connections to greater Judaism, saw this commandment as incumbent upon all believers. Clement of Alexandria writes that it is "right not to take usury for money, but with open hands and heart to bestow on those who need" (*Stromata* 2:18). Likewise both Tertullian and the *Apostolic Constitutions* speak against charging usury.[113] The obligation upon Gentile believers not to charge interest on loans must have been passed on from apostolic authority. Even in the Middle Ages, Christians did not charge interest on loans made to other Christians.

THE TEMPLE AND SACRIFICES

There are other obligations placed upon Gentiles that are not addressed in the Acts 15 decision, nor would they be included in the "duh … obvious" category either. They can rather be derived from a careful reading of the New Testament in light of Jewish thought. One such set of commandments is the Gentile's responsibility to honor the Temple. Leviticus 19:30 commands "You shall … reverence my sanctuary." This is observed not only by having a sense of holy fear and awe when one enters the sanctuary but also by respecting the different levels of sanctity that exist within the Temple. A regular Israelite was not permitted to go everywhere a Levite could go; a Levite was not permitted to go everywhere a priest could go; and the priest was not permitted to go everywhere the high priest could go. Everyone had their specific roles and functions, and the same was true for non-Jews.

Non-Jews were restricted to the outer court and could not pass beyond the *soreg*, which was the balustrade made of stone latticework that marked the barrier for the Court of the Gentiles.[114] While this may seem harsh, it was equally forbidden for the regular Israelite to enter into the area of priests and for the priests to enter into the Holy of Holies. The Apostle Paul was once accused of bringing a non-Jew past the Court of the Gentiles:

"Men of Israel, help! This is the man who is teaching everyone everywhere against the people and the law and this place. Moreover, he even brought Greeks into the temple and has defiled this holy place." For they had previously seen Trophimus the Ephesian with him in the city, and they supposed that Paul had brought him into the temple. (Acts 21:28–29)

Luke's narrative emphasizes that this was a false accusation made on faulty assumptions. The implication is that Paul would not have done so. Later Paul states unequivocally: "Neither against the law of the Jews, nor against the temple … have I committed any offense" (Acts 25:8). Paul actually honored the Temple practice of maintaining a distinctive area for those from the nations. By staying within the Court of the Gentiles, non-Jews kept the commandment to reverence the sanctuary and acting within the God-given role they played with regard to the Temple's sanctity.

HaShem declares that the Temple should be "a house of prayer for all people" and that "their burnt offerings and their sacrifices will be accepted on my altar" (Isaiah 56:7). If non-Jews do not come and worship at the Temple, then the service there is no longer complete. In the same way, if the regular Israelites or the priests themselves did not show up, the Temple could not fill its purpose without Gentiles. The sages of Israel recognized the Torah's inclusiveness for Gentiles within the Temple, even with regard to the sacrifices.

> For it was taught: [It would have sufficed had Scripture stated] "a man" (Leviticus 22:18), why does it state "a man, a man"? To include gentiles, that they may bring either votive or freewill-offerings like an Israelite. (b.*Menachot* 73b)[115]

While Gentiles were not to bring certain offerings such as guilt (*asham*, אשם) or sin (*chatat*, חטאת) offerings at certain times, they were permitted and encouraged to bring burnt (*olah*, עולה) and peace (*shlamim*, שלמים) offerings.[116] The priest would attend to these offerings just as if an Israelite offered them up, and Gentiles were required to follow the same standard requirements for the sacrifices, e.g., their sacrifices were to be unblemished (Leviticus 22:21) and from an animal seven days or older (Leviticus 22:27).[117]

We also find allusions in Paul's epistles to tithing which, like sacrifices, was a key component of the Temple.[118]

> And not only the creation, but we ourselves, who have the firstfruits of the Spirit, groan inwardly as we wait eagerly for adoption as sons, the redemption of our bodies. (Romans 8:23)

> If the dough offered as first fruits is holy, so is the whole lump, and if the root is holy, so are the branches. (Romans 11:16)

Paul mentions the mitzvah of *challah* (חלה), the commandment where a portion of the first of the dough is given to the priest every year, and also *bikkurim* ("firstfruits," בכורים), the injunction to bring a portion of the first crops to the Temple. Once again, while both of these are alluded to in a metaphorical sense, these analogies would only make sense if they were based on actual practice. This is supported by the fact that the *Didache* dedicates an entire section to instructing Gentile believers in tithing where the phrase "according to the commandment" appears twice.[119]

When surveying the New Testament, we see that the early believing community had an intense respect and connection to the Holy Temple in Jerusalem. They could actually be called a "Temple sect." This reverence was passed on to the new Gentile converts. Rather than being seen as a mere afterthought or as a group on the sideline, non-Jews were an integral part of what took place in the Temple. When they accept this role and honor the commandments surrounding it, they are not only honoring the Temple-related commandments that directly apply to them but they are honoring the totality of the hundred-plus commandments that are connected to the Temple. In that sense, they are actually keeping all of them.

CLEAN AND UNCLEAN

Intimately connected to the laws of the Temple and sacrifice are the laws of ritual purity, i.e., clean (*tahor*, טהור) and unclean (*tamei*, טמא). In fact, without a Temple today, most of the laws of clean and unclean are not applicable even to Jews. To a certain extent, all Jews are in a state of *tamei* today because the ritual mechanism for purification (ashes of a red heifer) is no longer available.

Jewish law declares that the Torah's twenty-plus commandments surrounding ritual purity are never applicable to Gentiles, whether there is a Temple standing or not. The sages based this on their meticulous reading of the Torah's text. The Torah introduces many of the purity injunctions with "Speak to the people of Israel" (e.g., Leviticus 15:2, 12:2). They reasoned: "The people of Israel are the subject of these matters and not Gentiles" (*Sifra, Tazria* 1:1).[120] Although this is the prevailing rabbinic opinion today, it appears that the apostles did not fully agree, and they extended purity concerns to the Gentile believers.

According to the book of Acts, early on when Gentiles began coming to faith in Messiah, the initial pressing issue was whether or not they could be considered ritually clean. This is the whole reason for Peter's vision of the sheet and his trip to Cornelius's house in Acts 10. Therefore there seems to have been serious concern over the ritual purity status of Gentiles coming into faith in Messiah.

The Master himself commands his Jewish followers to go and make disciples from all the nations, and the initial sign of their conversion is immersion (Matthew 28:19). Baptism in the church today has lost most of its Jewish symbolism. In first-century Judaism, immersion (*tevilah*, טבילה) was directly connected with ritual purity. While certainly immersion has a symbolic meaning as well, one always immerses to remove ritual impurity. Thus, the fact that Gentiles were required to immerse in order to become disciples of Yeshua shows that they were in some sense moving from a state of *tamei* into a state of *tahor*. Therefore, the Torah's laws of ritual purity must, in some sense, apply to non-Jewish disciples. They have become sanctified Gentiles. There is even a tradition that Peter himself would not eat with Gentiles unless they repented and were immersed.[121] It is noteworthy that rabbinic law does not prescribe immersion for Gentiles except upon conversion to Judaism.

We can even find indications that Gentile believers kept a level of purity commandments based on some of the moral injunctions of the Apostle Paul in his letters to the Corinthians. For example:

Therefore go out from their midst, and be separate from them, says the Lord, and touch no unclean thing; then I will welcome you. (2 Corinthians 6:17)

Since we have these promises, beloved, let us cleanse ourselves from every defilement of body and spirit, bringing holiness to completion in the fear of God. (2 Corinthians 7:1)

Expressions like "touch nothing unclean" and "let us cleanse ourselves from every defilement," while used by Paul in a metaphorical, homiletic sense, are based on the purity rubrics of the Torah. For these sayings to make sense to Gentile readers, they had to have some basis in the actual application of these laws. Paul touches on themes of clean and unclean once again in regard to mixed marriages between pagans and believers:

> For the unbelieving husband is made holy because of his wife, and the unbelieving wife is made holy because of her husband. Otherwise your children would be unclean, but as it is, they are holy. (1 Corinthians 7:14)

Here, Paul seems to cross the line between using the clean and unclean laws in a "spiritual" sense and quoting outright purity halachah for Gentiles. In 1 Corinthians 15:29, he speaks of "being baptized on behalf of the dead," which refers to the Torah's process of ritual purification after coming in contact with a dead body (*tum'at ha-met*, טומאת המת).[122] In a letter to a mixed community of Jews and Gentiles, his wording seems to imply that he sees both groups as obligated to these laws of purity.

Further evidence for Gentile believers following purity halachah can be found in early church literature. The *Didache* gives specific instructions regarding the initial immersion of the new Gentile believer:

> And concerning baptism, baptize this way ... in living water. But if you have no living water, baptize into other water; and if you cannot do so in cold water, do so in warm. But if you have neither, pour out water three times upon the head. (*Didache* 7)

The *Didache*'s instructions about immersing in "living water" correspond to the rabbinic requirement of *mayim chayim* (מים חיים). This requirement was seen as so essential to all immersions that if a natural body of water could not be found, specially constructed ritual baths were created called *mikva'ot* (מקואות) to collect living water. Although the *Didache* allows for alternatives under certain circumstances, the ideal way to immerse was in *mayim chayim*. Early Christian baptismal pools found in "Israel, Turkey, Greece, and Rome were built on the same principle as mikva'ot."[123] The *Canons of Hippolytus* gives similar instructions about "living water" and adds that one must remove anything that hinders complete contact with the water, including clothing and jewelry—instructions in complete accordance with rabbinic law.[124]

There is also the early church practice of washing one's hands before prayer, which echoes the Jewish practice that was done in imitation of priestly purity regulations before offering sacrifices.[125]

> So fixed became this custom of washing the hands before divine service that the Christian Church adopted the Jewish custom of providing the worshipers with fountains or basins of water.[126]

All of this evidence points to early Gentile believers observing some level of purity halachah. However, the actual specifics of a Gentile believer's obligation to purity laws is difficult to assess and certainly beyond the scope of this book. (For that matter, the actual specifics of a Jewish person's obligation to purity laws outside of a Temple context are equally difficult to assess.) While this becomes a moot point in light of the destruction of the Temple, it is certainly something that will need to be considered for the Messianic kingdom. After all, the book of Revelation tells us that "nothing unclean will ever enter" the New Jerusalem (Revelation 21:27).

SET-TIME PRAYERS

Another outgrowth of the Temple commandments was the concept of prescribed daily times of prayer. Prayer itself is one of the 613 commandments.[127] The Torah states: "Serve the LORD your God with all your heart" (Deuteronomy 10:12). The sages ask, "What is the Service of the Heart? Prayer."[128] "Service" in this passage is the word *avodah* (עבודה), which is also used to describe the priests' duties in the Temple. Thus there remains a close connection between prayer and the Temple.

Furthermore, Numbers 28:1 states that the daily offerings of the Temple were to take place at the "appointed time" (*mo'ed*, מועד), a phrase that is also used in connection with the feasts. Thus the twice-daily times of sacrifice, morning and afternoon (to which were eventually added a third time for recitation of the evening *shma*) became times of *avodah*, not just for the priests in the Temple but for the regular Israelite as well. Therefore, in the Jewish mindset, the Torah's obligation to pray is specifically fulfilled by praying at the daily times of sacrifice.

The Apostle Paul exhorts Gentile believers to "pray without ceasing" (1 Thessalonians 5:17), "be constant in prayer" (Romans 12:12), and "continue steadfastly in prayer" (Colossians 4:2). All of these passages imply that Paul considered the Torah's commandment to pray as incumbent upon Gentile believers. They also imply close connection to the daily sacrifice in the Temple, which was called the *korban tamid* (קרבן תמיד), which means "continual offering" (Numbers 28:6).

We find Cornelius the God-fearer praying at these set times.

> At Caesarea there was a man named Cornelius, a centurion of what was known as the Italian Cohort, a devout man who feared God with all his household, gave alms generously to the people, and prayed continually to God. About the ninth hour of the day he saw clearly in a vision an angel of God come in and say to him, "Cornelius." (Acts 10:1–3)

The "ninth hour" would correspond to the time of the afternoon sacrifice. As a Gentile, Cornelius was joining in with greater Israel at these appointed times of prayer. Once again turning to the *Didache,* which was written as a manual of living for Gentile believers, we find the injunction to pray the Lord's prayer "three times each day"[129] corresponding to the three daily times of prayer in Judaism: *shacharit* (שחרית) in the morning, *minchah* (מנחה) in the afternoon, and *ma'ariv* (מעריב) in the evening. Given the early date of composition for the document (first century CE) and the purported connection to the twelve apostles, it indicates that the early Gentile believers were indeed praying at the set times along with the rest of Israel. It appears as well that they did not just consider it a voluntary action but as a bounden duty. It should also be noted that the primary prayer in Jewish tradition recited at the set times of prayer was the *Shmoneh Esreh,* and it is not surprising that fragments and reworkings of this prayer appear in church literature.[130] Moreover, outside of Protestant evangelicalism, most Christians in the world today still observe set times of prayer. Christian liturgical traditions, whether Greek Orthodox, Syriac, Coptic, or Roman Catholic, all trace the set hours of Christian prayer back to Jewish practice.[131]

MEALTIME BLESSINGS

Not only were Gentile believers participating in set-time prayers along with the rest of Judaism, but they were also following the Torah's injunction to bless HaShem at meal times. Deuteronomy 8:10 tells the children of Israel, "And you shall eat and be full, and you shall bless the LORD your God." Judaism interpreted that commandment as the obligation to say a blessing of thanksgiving after the meal, referred to as "blessing for the food (*birkat ha-mazon,* ברכת המזון)." The blessing thanks God for the food that has just been eaten. By extension, the sages also enjoined that one make a short blessing before the meal as well. They cite Psalm 24:1:

> Rab Judah said in the name of Samuel: To enjoy anything of this world without a benediction is like making personal use of things consecrated to heaven, since it says: "The earth is the Lord's and the fullness thereof." (b.*Brachot* 35a)[132]

In the mind of the sages, to experience a benefit from something without first giving thanks to God shows ingratitude; or even worse, it is like stealing from HaShem by causing something holy to become profane, since everything belongs to him.

In Paul's discussion in 1 Corinthians of the prohibition of eating meat sacrificed to idols, he too cites Psalm 24:1 and in a similar fashion.[133] The citation of this verse would only make sense for Paul's primarily non-Jewish readership if they were reciting pre-meal blessings and were aware of the rabbinic interpretation of the verse. He tells them to "partake with thankfulness" and says of himself, "I give thanks" (1 Corinthians 10:30). In other words, they were reciting pre-meal *brachot* ("blessings," ברכות).

Paul also refers to the practice of the *birkat ha-mazon* in his discussion of the Last Supper. It is customary in some circles to include a cup of wine in the after-meal blessing, and this cup is referred to as the *kos shel brachah* ("cup of blessing," כוס של ברכה).[134] Paul refers specifically to the name of this cup when he states: "Is not the cup of blessing which we bless a sharing in the blood of Christ?" (1 Corinthians 10:16). Once again, this type of imagery would only make sense to an audience who was already familiar with the practice and the vocabulary.

As was the case with the daily times of prayer, the *Didache* instructs the Gentiles to follow the Torah by reciting mealtime blessings. The document presents specific, liturgical prayers for Gentiles to recite before and after meals.[135] Scholars have noted the similarity in form and wording between the *Didache* mealtime prayers and the traditional *brachot* and *birkat ha-mazon*.[136] All of this evidence points to the fact that Gentile believers felt commanded to bless HaShem at mealtimes both before and after they eat.

THE SIGN COMMANDMENTS

Even when we examine the sign commandments of the Torah and markers of Jewish identity which are not incumbent on Gentiles, the Gentile believers are not completely off the hook. The sign (*ot*, אות) commandments are those which the Torah explicitly designates as a distinguishing mark of the Jewish people: Shabbat[137], tefillin[138], circumcision[139], and by extension mezuzah (which is included in the passages about tefillin)[140] and tzitzit (which Israel is called to "look upon and remember")[141]. These are all commandments that distinguish Israel from the nations around them.[142] We will discuss the God-fearing Gentile believers' relationship to these commandments in detail in later chapters.

Although the Gentile disciples are not specifically commanded to "guard" these sign commandments in the sense of observing them, they do need to "guard" them in the sense of protecting them. For example, take the mitzvah of circumcision (*brit milah*, ברית מילה). The apostles clearly do not bind this sign of the covenant upon Gentile believers, but say that they are to help protect this mitzvah by not blurring the lines of distinction. Paul states:

> Was anyone at the time of his call already circumcised? Let him not seek to remove the marks of circumcision. Was anyone at the time of his call uncircumcised? Let him not seek circumcision. (1 Corinthians 7:18)

Gentiles are specifically enjoined not to be circumcised for the ritual covenantal status. Interestingly enough, the Rambam also wrote about Gentiles and circumcision. After explaining that it is forbidden according to Jewish law for a Jew to circumcise a Gentile for medical purposes, he writes: "If, however, the gentile intends to fulfill the mitzvah of circumcision, it is a mitzvah to circumcise him." [143] We can assume that, like Maimonides, the apostles would have no problem with Gentiles voluntarily being circumcised for the sake of the mitzvah, but to do so complete with expectation of covenantal status as Jews would be to "seek circumcision" in the Pauline sense.

We will examine more of these sign commandments and the Gentiles' relationship to them in the next three chapters.

COMMANDANTS FOR ALL

Just like Jews, Gentile believers were expected to take up the commandments of the Torah incumbent upon them and live a kingdom lifestyle full of ethical concerns, moral considerations, and ritual practices. In short, the Gentile believers practiced Judaism along with the Jewish believers, albeit as it applied to them as non-Jews. All of God's people have a specific role within his kingdom, and we all have commandments that we are required to carry out in order to live a life of holiness in a manner worthy of our Master.

Although we have covered quite a number of the commandments to which Gentile believers in Yeshua are obligated, this is by no means a conclusive study or a complete list of those commandments.[144] Instead, my intention in this chapter has been to demonstrate that, aside from a few "sign" commandments and specific identity markers unique to the Jewish people, the apostles and the earliest believing community considered Gentiles under obligation to almost all of the rest of the commandments of the Torah, in one fashion or another. In fact, even in the case of commandments that Gentiles are specifically not obligated to keep, the Scriptures place expectations upon the Gentile believers to protect those commandments for the Jewish people.

This raises the question, "What about the Sabbath?" How did God-fearers relate to the Sabbath, and how should God-fearing Gentile believers guard the Sabbath? Some voices within Judaism and Messianic Judaism try to deter Gentiles from any type of Sabbath observance. What was the apostolic practice?

CHAPTER FIVE

SHABBAT AND THE GENTILE

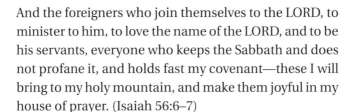

> And the foreigners who join themselves to the LORD, to minister to him, to love the name of the LORD, and to be his servants, everyone who keeps the Sabbath and does not profane it, and holds fast my covenant—these I will bring to my holy mountain, and make them joyful in my house of prayer. (Isaiah 56:6–7)

Secular Zionist Asher Ginzberg once said, "More than the Jewish people have kept the Sabbath, the Sabbath has kept the Jewish people." The observance of Sabbath by Jews for thousands of years has kept the Jewish people together throughout their tumultuous history. The concept of taking one day off in seven is unparalleled in the ancient Near East.[145] The Sabbath remains one of the greatest innovations of the Bible and the hallmark of Jewish religious life.

Shabbat not only provides a day of rest from the chaos of this world but affords every Jew the opportunity to recharge his spiritual battery and connect with the Divine. It allows one to stay focused on that which is important and lasting, that which truly matters. The work week does not become an end unto itself but a means to reach the holiest day. Exodus 31 also tells us that Shabbat is a covenantal sign of the unique relationship between HaShem and the Jewish people.

That's all good for Jews, but is there a Sabbath rest for God-fearing Gentile believers in Messiah? Can Gentile believers observe the Sabbath and receive the blessings that come with it without trampling on the unique calling that God has placed on the Jewish people? In this chapter we will discover that there is a place for those of the nations who have joined themselves to Israel to partake in the Sabbath rest.

THE SEVENTH DAY

Thousands of years before the Torah is given to Israel at Mount Sinai, God lays the foundation of Shabbat by resting on the seventh day himself:

> Thus the heavens and the earth were finished, and all the host of them. And on the seventh day God finished his work that he had done, and he rested on the seventh day from all his work that he had done. So God blessed the seventh day and made it holy, because on it God rested from all his work that he had done in creation. (Genesis 2:1–3)

The noun "Shabbat" (שבת) is not present in the text of Genesis 2, even though the verbal form *shavat* (שבת) does appear twice. Although the name "Shabbat" is not explicitly mentioned, nor is the Genesis 2 narrative in command form, the meaning is clear: HaShem not only institutes the seventh day as a day of rest but he declares the day as blessed and sanctified. The Sabbath has been set apart as special from all other days. In the words of Nahum Sarna, God imbues the day with "an extraordinary vital power that communicates itself in a beneficial way." [146] In the first six days of creation God established his dominion over space, and now through the Sabbath he establishes dominion over time. The day connects man with sacred time, while at the same time reminding him that his productivity has limits.

Rabbi Chaim ben Attar (1746–1793) in his *Or HaChaim*, explains that a less-literal reading of the text can be homiletically said to reveal that the very soul of creation was imparted on Shabbat. He brings in Exodus 31:17 which reads: "On the seventh day he rested and was refreshed." "Refreshed" in Hebrew is *vayinnafash* (וינפש) and contains the word *nefesh* (נפש), usually translated "soul," which is from the same root, *nafash*. Playing on this meaning of *nefesh*, Rabbi Attar comments:

> On the Sabbath day G-d created the "soul" of the world
> … The plain meaning is undoubtedly that *Shabbat vay-innafash*, because He rested on the Sabbath and with
> it the soul arrived. This means that all creatures were
> granted an abundance of vitality, something they had
> lacked previously.[147]

In Rabbi Attar's opinion, all of creation—human, beast, vegetation, and even inorganic material—benefits from the holiness of the Sabbath. According to him, since time began, throughout all generations there have always been those righteous individuals who kept the Sabbath to one extent or another.[148] It started with the first man Adam, then Seth, Methuselah, Noah, Shem, all the way to Abraham, who became the father of Israel.[149] The midrash imagines that Adam himself composed Psalm 92, "a song for the Sabbath day."[150] Therefore, in the opinions of the sages of Israel, the Sabbath was carried by non-Jews a long while before the baton was handed to the Jewish people.

A SIGN BETWEEN GOD AND ISRAEL

The Sabbath becomes an explicit commandment and a sign between God and the Jewish people only after God delivers Israel from Egypt.

> And the LORD said to Moses, "You are to speak to the
> people of Israel and say, 'Above all you shall keep my Sab-
> baths, for this is a sign between me and you throughout
> your generations, that you may know that I, the LORD,
> sanctify you … It is a sign forever between me and the
> people of Israel that in six days the LORD made heaven
> and earth, and on the seventh day he rested and was
> refreshed.'" (Exodus 31:12–13, 17)

The Sabbath is the seal of the covenant that God made with Israel on Mount Sinai, and its observance is the "sign" (*ot,* אות) of the unique relationship that God has with the people of Israel. Rashi comments on these verses:

It is a great sign between us that I chose you through My allotting My day of rest for your rest … That is for the nations to know through it "that I am HaShem Who sanctifies you."[151]

God set Israel apart from all other nations and has chosen that nation to bear his name to the rest of the world. An ancient midrash comments: "For this is a sign between me and you—and not between me and the nations of the world" (*Mechilta* to Exodus 31:12). The Sabbath is one of the most definitive, distinctive identity-markers of the entire Torah.

The Sabbath "sign of the covenant" includes observing the numerous Sabbath prohibitions found in the Torah which the sages later classified into thirty-nine prohibitions. None of these stipulations are found in the Genesis narrative where the universal Shabbat principle is introduced. Rabbi Elchanan Adler comments on Sabbath observance within the context of the unique relationship of Israel to HaShem:

A halakhic Sabbath observance … can be deemed a threat to that relationship when emulated by a non-Jew.[152]

According to this opinion, the observance of Shabbat in a strict halachic Jewish sense is a unique requirement and distinction that applies to Israel alone.

But even in the Exodus 31 narrative we get a sense that there is another aspect to the Sabbath. Not only is it a sign of God's sanctification of Israel, i.e., the Exodus from Egypt, which is, of course, a uniquely Jewish experience, but the Sabbath is also a sign "that in six days the LORD made heaven and earth, and on the seventh day he rested and was refreshed," which is a universal experience. In that way, the Sabbath retains its original meaning from Genesis as well as taking on the narrower covenantal context with Israel. These two distinct purposes are confirmed when we examine Shabbat in the two accounts of the Ten Commandments:

You shall remember that you were a slave in the land of Egypt, and the LORD your God brought you out from there with a mighty hand and an outstretched arm. Therefore the LORD your God commanded you to keep (*shamar,* שמר) the Sabbath day. (Deuteronomy 5:15)

Remember (*zachar,* זכר) the Sabbath day, to keep it holy … For in six days the LORD made heaven and earth, the sea, and all that is in them, and rested the seventh day. Therefore the LORD blessed the Sabbath day and made it holy. (Exodus 20:8, 11)

In the context of the Exodus from Egypt, the injunction is to "keep" or guard the Sabbath, whereas in the context of creation, the injunction is to "remember" the Sabbath. Sabbath therefore serves dual intentions. Is it possible then that there are two different levels or aspects to Shabbat observance? Some of the sages indeed felt that because certain aspects of Shabbat are pre-Sinai, all mankind were obligated to "remember" the Sabbath:

Thus it says [in the Decalogue], "Remember the Shabbos day," indicating that even those who do not observe [Shabbos by refraining from work] are at least included in [the commandment of] remembering [Shabbos]. All the nations are obligated to remember the Shabbos day in order to implant in their hearts belief in creation ex nihilo [since Shabbos is a sign that God created the world] which bears witness that God's testimony to His existence is trustworthy, since included in the seven Noachide commandments is [the commandment] that they should not worship idols. (*Kli Yakar* to Exodus 28:7 [Levine])

In this regard, the Sabbath is a "sign" commandment for the Jewish people and the Jewish people are obligated to keep the Sabbath, but it also carries aspects of observance and remembrance that are pertinent to Gentiles.

THE GER TOSHAV

We find another example of the relationship between Gentiles and Shabbat in the Torah's injunction that the non-Jewish alien is not permitted to be used as a worker on Shabbat.

Six days you shall do your work, but on the seventh day you shall rest; that your ox and your donkey may have rest, and the son of your servant woman, and the alien, may be refreshed. (Exodus 23:12)

We examined this passage briefly in chapter two from a literal perspective, but now let's examine the passage in light of traditional rabbinic interpretation. The rabbis viewed the "alien (*ger*)" in this passage as not referring to a full convert but rather to the *ger toshav* ("resident alien," גר תושב).[153] A *ger toshav* is a Gentile who lived among Israel within the land. They were, therefore, under the legal protection of Israel, including the receipt of charity if necessary.[154]

Based upon that interpretation of the *ger* as a non-Jewish resident among the people of Israel, Exodus 23:12 provides another example of Gentile participation in Shabbat. Commenting on this passage, Rashi goes so far as to say that the Torah obligates the resident alien to keep Shabbat.[155] At the same time though, it is widely accepted that Sabbath restrictions for the *ger toshav* are less stringent than for the Israelite.

> It has been taught: A resident alien may do work for him-
> self on the Sabbath in the same measure as an Israelite
> may do on the intermediate days of the festivals. R. Akiba
> says: As an Israelite on the festival. R. Jose says: A resident
> alien may do work for himself on the Sabbath in the same
> measure as an Israelite on week-days. R .Simeon says:
> Both a resident alien and a male or female sojourning
> heathen slave may do work for themselves in the same
> measure as an Israelite may do on week-days. (b.*Kritot* 9a)

Therefore, while the *ger toshav* seems to have been under an obligation to keep Shabbat, it was a much looser obligation than that of the Jewish person.

As a whole, the category of the *ger toshav* is difficult to define precisely. According to most halachic authorities, this classification of Gentiles is not applicable today because it is contingent upon the observance of the Jubilee year.[156] However, there are some halachists who believe that the category of the *ger toshav* can be used to justify Gentile Shabbat observance today.[157]

ISAIAH 56

One of the most commonly cited passages in the Tanach to justify a Gentile's observance of the Sabbath is Isaiah 56.[158] Here we read of God's promises to eunuchs and foreigners, that they too can find a place among the Jewish people.

> Let not the foreigner who has joined himself to the LORD say, "The LORD will surely separate me from his people"; and let not the eunuch say, "Behold, I am a dry tree." For thus says the LORD: "To the eunuchs who keep my Sabbaths, who choose the things that please me and hold fast my covenant, I will give in my house and within my walls a monument and a name better than sons and daughters; I will give them an everlasting name that shall not be cut off. And the foreigners who join themselves to the LORD, to minister to him, to love the name of the LORD, and to be his servants, everyone who keeps the Sabbath and does not profane it, and holds fast my covenant—these I will bring to my holy mountain, and make them joyful in my house of prayer; their burnt offerings and their sacrifices will be accepted on my altar; for my house shall be called a house of prayer for all peoples." (Isaiah 56:3–7)

Gentiles and eunuchs are discussed together because the two groups have something in common in that they are both outside of the community of Israel—the eunuch because of the law in Deuteronomy 23:1 and the Gentile because he is not Jewish. Yet in the prophecy, HaShem seeks to alleviate these anxieties by promising to reward both the eunuch and the non-Jew who voluntarily take on the observance of the Sabbath. Rabbi Rabinowitz writes: "The underlying message is that being God's servant is not dependent upon having Jewish forebears, or upon one's continued lineage among the Jewish People."[159]

The rabbis are unanimous in interpreting this passage as referring only to those Gentiles who undergo a proselyte conversion and become Jewish. That is to say, the Gentiles from "all nations" first become Jewish and then attain access to the Temple and the sacrificial services.

The apostles may have understood the reference to the Gentile in this prophecy in the same way, that is, as referring to a formal proselyte, because it says that the Gentile will "hold fast my covenant."[160] Yet there is another way of viewing the Gentile in this passage. *The New International Commentary on the Old Testament* brings out the spirit of this passage:

> What matters is that they keep my Sabbaths, choose that in which I delight, and lay hold of my covenant. These people are on God's side. They love what he loves, hate what he hates, want what he wants. They do not keep the Sabbaths because they must or [else] they will be destroyed. They keep them because they are the Lord's Sabbaths. Their behavior is an expression of a relationship. This is what God longs for in his people, and if anyone will do this, their parentage or their body has nothing to do with their acceptability.[161]

Contrary to the traditional interpretation, we should probably not consider the Gentiles discussed in Isaiah 56 as full, legal proselytes who have become Jewish. If they were, then there would be nothing remarkable about their being gathered with Israel or given privileges in the Temple, nor could the Temple then be called a "house of prayer for all peoples." The full proselyte leaves behind his identity in a foreign nation. If all Gentiles must become Jewish before entering the Messianic Temple, then it should not be called "a house of prayer for all peoples."

Therefore, the Isaiah 56 Gentiles must be real Gentiles who have maintained a distinct, non-Jewish identity and yet taken a place with the nation of Israel. They voluntarily choose to observe the Sabbath along with Israel.

Perhaps we should place these Gentiles in the larger context of the preceding passages. In chapter 55, HaShem speaks of his Servant the Messiah, saying, "Behold, I made him a witness to the peoples, a leader and commander for the peoples." Then he addresses the Messiah directly, saying, "Behold, you shall call a nation that you do not know, and a nation that did not know you shall run to you" (Isaiah 55:4–5).

Therefore we should understand the Sabbath-keeping Gentiles who join themselves to the God of Israel, to minister to him and to love the name of HaShem, to be his servants and keep his covenant, as the Messiah's Gentiles. The description fits the God-fearing Gentile believers who have run to take shelter under the King of Israel. In turn, Isaiah 56 establishes precedence for Gentiles in Messiah honoring Shabbat—not because they have to, but because they want to.

IN THE SYNAGOGUE

Let's now turn to the New Testament. It is obvious from the Gospels and the book of Acts that the Master and the early Jewish disciples had a high regard for the commandment of Shabbat. The New Testament contains no hint of the Sabbath being switched from Saturday to Sunday.[162] There is no more telling a passage than what we read right after Yeshua is crucified: "On the Sabbath they rested according to the commandment" (Luke 23:56). At the pinnacle of their grief and sorrow, these faithful disciples observed the commandment of Sabbath rest just as their Master had taught them. For the Jewish believer in Messiah, Sabbath observance was and is a given.

As for Gentiles, the Jerusalem Council in Acts 15 laid out four essential obligations for new believers from the nations. So, while the council did not bind Gentiles to the Sabbath, they most certainly would not have prohibited them from choosing to rest on Sabbath.[163] The believing Gentile's participation in the Sabbath, along with the rest of the Jewish community, may underlie this curious postscript to the Acts 15 decision:

> For from ancient generations Moses has had in every city those who proclaim him, for he is read every Sabbath in the synagogues. (Acts 15:21)

This oft-argued text might indicate that the Gentile converts attended synagogue along with their fellow Jewish brethren. In fact, we see evidence throughout the book of Acts of Gentile believers attending synagogue.[164] This seems to be a general assumption of the apostolic community and it is relevant to the discussion, because synagogue attendance is one of the hallmarks of Sabbath observance. One would assume, at a bare minimum the Gentile participating in the synagogue did not work on Saturdays. Gentile participation in the synagogue is, in and of itself, evidence that some Gentile believers did observe the seventh-day Sabbath to some degree. Berndt Schaller writes:

> The primitive Christian community largely kept the Sabbath, more strictly in the case of Jewish Christians, but in fact that of some Gentile Christians as well.[165]

Thus Gentile believers, while not keeping the Sabbath as strictly as their Jewish brethren, were "remembering Shabbat" in their own right and would not have even thought to ignore God's holy day as most believers do today. There is actually evidence from Josephus and other classical writers that Sabbath observance was widespread among non-Jews in general throughout the Roman Empire.[166] Apparently, many of these so-called "God-fearers" found benefit and blessing in ceasing and resting on the seventh day.

On the flip side, Paul makes it abundantly clear in his letter to the Colossians that Gentiles are not to be judged or condemned on the basis of their Shabbat observance and halachah.[167] This letter was addressed primarily to non-Jewish believers in Yeshua:

> Therefore let no one pass judgment on you in questions of food and drink, or with regard to a festival or a new moon or a Sabbath. These are a shadow of the things to come, but the substance belongs to Christ. (Colossians 2:16–17)

Sabbath observance was a unique sign of God's relationship with Israel proper and therefore could not be imposed upon Gentile believers, despite the fact that those Gentiles had come to share a spiritual inheritance in Israel. Nevertheless, these instructions of Paul should not be seen as forbidding a Gentile from observing the Sabbath. Shabbat observance was not obligatory, but it was certainly not forbidden. The Gentile believers needed a holy day of rest and worship just as the Jewish believers did. As members of the greater commonwealth of Israel, the Sabbath was open to them, and was, in fact, the obvious (and only) choice.

FROM SHABBAT TO SUNDAY

Although Jewish believers continued to be faithful in their practice of Sabbath observance, Sabbatarianism did not last long for the majority of the believing Gentiles. There were holdouts such as the "Ethiopian Orthodox Church, Jacobites, and Thomas Christians; Oriental Orthodox Churches," who continued to observe a seventh-day Sabbath beyond the first century.[168] In fact some scholars believe that some Gentile believers were still attending synagogues on the Sabbath perhaps as late as the sixth century CE.[169] Yet, for the most part, Gentile Christianity began to neglect the Sabbath as early as the late first century. How did this happen so quickly? Several scholars reconstruct a logical progression.[170]

The first day of the week (Sunday) began to be honored by believers very early on in the development of the faith. Christians marked the first day (alongside of the Sabbath) because of the significance of associations with both the resurrection and the giving of the Spirit. In fact we even find subtle evidence of a nascent first-day practice in the New Testament, albeit it is more likely believers originally met Saturday night after the Sabbath when travel, carrying, and cooking restrictions were lifted and they could commemorate the resurrection.[171] Among Gentile believers, observance of the seventh day began to fade, perhaps due to the fact that it grew cumbersome to honor both days. As the Gentile Christian community became severed from the synagogue, Sabbath practice seemed unnecessary and irrelevant. Hostility toward Judaism and a reluctance to be identified as Jews during the tumultuous years between the two Jewish revolts made Gentiles reluctant to be associated with the Sabbath.[172] By the end of the first century, Gentile Christians openly opposed believers who still kept Sabbath. Hostility toward Sabbatarians was heightened by the increasing desire of Gentile believers to make a formal break from Judaism. As early as 105 CE, Ignatius declares that Christians are "no longer keeping the Sabbath but living in obedience to the Lord's Day [i.e., Sunday]."[173] Within a short period of time, the practice became universal in Gentile churches and the switch became all but canonized.

There were other factors at work here as well. There was not only the increasing desire for Christians to separate from Jews but a desire by Jews to separate from Christians. Here's what the Talmud says about Gentiles keeping Shabbat:

> Resh Lakish also said: "A heathen who keeps a day of rest, deserves death, for it is written, 'And a day and a night they shall not rest' (Genesis 8:22), and a master has said: 'Their prohibition is their death sentence.'" Rabina said: "Even if he rested on a Monday." (b.*Sanhedrin* 58b)

The death penalty is not meant literally (the synagogue had no such authority in the Talmudic era) but rather expresses the severity with which the sages viewed this transgression.[174] Nevertheless there is a strong desire on the part of the sages to discourage Gentiles from keeping Shabbat. The reasons might have been two-fold: to keep Shabbat as a unique covenantal sign for Jews and at the same time a sense of irritation about Christians keeping Shabbat. A textual variant for this Talmudic passage has been found that contains the word *akkum* (עכו"ם) which actually denotes an idolater and not just a Gentile. Theodore Friedman writes:

> Probably when Resh Lakish stated that a gentile (*akkum,* etc., in existing texts) who observed the Sabbath is punishable by death, he had in mind Christians.[175]

Why would the Talmudic-era sages not want Christians to observe Shabbat? Bar Ilan professor Abraham Weiss proposes an interesting solution:

> From the 29th ordinance of the council of Laodicea we learn that at the time all the church members did not yet accept Sunday as the Sabbath-day and day of rest. Some of the members rested on the seventh day, and it appears that among these there were also some who thought that in keeping the Sabbath they were, so to speak, establishing closer contact with Judaism. The Church fought against those who rested on the Sabbath and sought ties with Judaism by excommunicating them.[176]

So the Talmud, along with the church, discouraged and even forbade Christian Gentiles from observing the Sabbath in order to create a cleaner distinction between the two religions and to prevent intermixing. When we add all these circumstances together, we can begin to get a picture of how Sabbath observance all but completely disappeared from the early Gentile church.

Although there have been small pockets of believers keeping a seventh-day Sabbath throughout history, such as the Transylvanian believers in the Late Middle Ages/Early Modern Period and even today with the Seventh-Day Adventists and Seventh-Day Baptists, almost all of Christendom favored Sunday over Sabbath. It is really only in our day and age that we see such a widespread trend of believing Gentiles returning to the seventh-day Sabbath. Indeed, we are attempting to resurrect something that had been lost for thousands of years.

OBSERVANCE WITH DISTINCTION

Before we draw some practical conclusions about Sabbath observance for God-fearing Gentile believers, here are four key points we have learned:

1. The principle of Sabbath was established in Genesis at creation and it was universal in scope.
2. The commandment of Sabbath was given exclusively to the Jewish people at Mount Sinai as a sign of Israel's unique relationship with HaShem.
3. There are two aspects to the commandment of Shabbat: "remembering" and "observing."
4. While the apostles did not bind the Sabbath on Gentile believers, many of the early non-Jewish believers voluntarily embraced the Sabbath as a natural outcome of their participation in Judaism and spiritual membership in the commonwealth of Israel.

As those of us who are Gentiles seek to go back to the faith and practice of the earliest God-fearing believers, many of us will be drawn into honoring the Sabbath on some level. In our observance of the Sabbath, it is important that we honor the Jewish people's unique relationship with the Sabbath.

Rav Yoel Schwartz, an expert in Jewish law as it relates to non-Jews, writes: "A [non-Jew] should not observe the Shabbat in the manner that a Jew does."[177] While at first glance many of us might balk at this, we have to remember that to Rabbi Schwartz full observance of Shabbat involves the full weight of the thirty-nine prohibitions of Shabbat halachah, including not using any electricity or driving in a car or even carrying an object in one's pocket. At the same time Rabbi Schwartz tries to find a balance between allowing Gentiles to receive the blessings of the Sabbath day and compromising the distinct sign of Israel. He goes on to say:

> There is room to suggest that the [Gentiles], even nowadays, by accepting to fulfill the seven commandments, are in the same category as a Ger Toshav ["resident alien"] and should, according to Rashi, be required or at least allowed to keep the Shabbat.[178]

Practically, he goes on to suggest a Sabbath day where Gentiles refrain from work, enjoy festive meals, and study Torah. Bear in mind, though, that he does not have believers in view and therefore takes no thought for how Gentile believers might relate more to a Jewish observance of the Sabbath. The *Chemdat Yisrael* even comments that "if a non-Jew were to commit himself exclusively to God, and ascribe influence to Him alone, it would be allowed and even fitting for him to rest on Shabbat like his Maker does."[179] Thus, there becomes a precedent for Gentiles "remembering" the Sabbath of Creation.

Gentiles in Messiah should feel free to honor the Shabbat and join in with the rest of Israel, even observing some of the customs of the Jewish people. After all, Shabbat was originally a universal expression. On the other hand, it may not be advisable for a Gentile to embrace a fully halachic observance of the Sabbath, especially outside of a Jewish community. At the same time, although a Gentile will probably not be observing all of the traditional stringencies which Jewish law places around the Sabbath, he should have respect for his Jewish brother who does.

Jew and Gentile both need to set aside a holy day for rest and sanctification. We need a time to connect both with our family and with God himself. Sabbath is the day we prepare for ahead of time, so all we are left to do is enjoy and delight in this precious gift. You might even say that as the world becomes more and more hectic and our lives become more and more busy, the practice of Shabbat becomes more and more important. Orthodox rabbi Shmuley Boteach envisions a time when many from all nations will begin to observe a seventh day of rest:

> In this epoch of cell phones, beepers, E-mail, and fax machines, humans are subjected to work and noise seven days a week, twenty-four hours a day. We are rarely afforded a moment of solitude. I predict that more and more people, Jews and non-Jews, will begin to embrace that particularly Jewish observance of the Sabbath as a way to quiet the clamor and to regain a sense of balance and peace. Get ready to see non-Jewish families setting aside one day a week in which they don't answer the telephone, rent videos, or surf the net. Modern-day amusements are as incarcerating as they are liberating, and we all need a break. Every Saturday will be designated as an uninterrupted family day, during which cell phones and Palm Pilots are switched off.[180]

May it be for the whole world! Yet, how much more so is this applicable to those of us from the nations who have been grafted into the olive tree of Israel through Messiah! As God-fearing Gentile believers, we can find solidarity with the first God-fearing believers who chose to observe Sabbath out of love for God and love for Israel. We can help spread the light of the universal principle of Sabbath, a principle in which all mankind can find benefit, goodness, holiness, and blessing.

Naturally, the discussion about God-fearing Gentiles honoring the weekly Sabbath raises the question, "What about the rest of the holy days?" Should Gentile believers keep the Jewish festivals? How should Gentile believers in Messianic Judaism relate to Passover, Pentecost, Rosh Hashanah, the Day of Atonement, and the festival of Tabernacles?

CHAPTER SIX

GENTILES AND THE FESTIVALS OF ISRAEL

◆—◆—◆

> After this I looked, and behold, a great multitude that
> no one could number, from every nation, from all tribes
> and peoples and languages, standing before the throne
> and before the Lamb, clothed in white robes, with palm
> branches in their hands, and crying out with a loud voice,
> "Salvation belongs to our God who sits on the throne, and
> to the Lamb!" (Revelation 7:9–10)

In the previous chapter we discussed Gentiles and the observance
of Shabbat. Shabbat is a sign commandment for Jewish people.
The rest of Israel's holy days are direct extensions of the Sabbath.
They too, in their own right, are part of the category of sign commandments. So what about non-Jewish believers participating in
the festivals of Israel? Much of the same argumentation that was
used for Shabbat can also be used for the festivals encouraging
Gentile participation. So rather than rehashing that, it might be
best to look historically at the practice of the early Jewish believers and what festivals and celebrations they were participating in.
While it can be taken for granted that the earliest Jewish followers
of Yeshua were celebrating and observing the biblical festivals
to their fullest, let's examine the evidence for Gentile believers
keeping the holy days during the first few centuries CE.

IN HONOR OF THE LORD

While Acts 15 makes no mention of the Jewish festivals being incumbent upon Gentile believers, we do find several references to Gentile believers celebrating Jewish festivals in the writings of Paul. As we pointed out in the last chapter, Paul is clear that Gentiles are not to be judged or condemned on the basis of their festival observance.

> Therefore let no one pass judgment on you in questions of food and drink, or with regard to a festival or a new moon or a Sabbath. These are a shadow of the things to come, but the substance belongs to Christ. (Colossians 2:16–17)

Paul's instructions, however, should not be seen as forbidding a Gentile from observing the appointed times of the Torah. In his essay, *Christians Observing Jewish Festivals of the Autumn*, Daniel Stökl Ben Ezra points out that Paul "does not prohibit observing Jewish festivals but only *coercing* Gentiles to observe these festivals."[181] Paul's instruction in Colossians can be understood as a prohibition on coercing a Gentile believer to keep the holy days, but it can also be read as a prohibition on judging a Gentile regarding the manner in which he did keep the holy days.

Ben Ezra reads the same concern for Gentile observance of the festivals and holy days in Paul's letter to the Romans 14:4–5 where Paul states one who chooses to "observe the day" does so "in honor of the Lord." From Ben Ezra's interpretation, these instructions should be understood as addressed to Gentile believers in Rome and not to Jewish believers. Ben Ezra comments:

> [Paul] assumes that some members of the Roman communities observe Jewish festivals and he gives them the freedom to do so. Paul even regards the observance of Yom Kippur and other days as worship if they are celebrated in honor of the Lord.[182]

So while Paul was adamant that Gentiles should not be forced to observe the Torah's festivals, at the same time he gave them complete permission and freedom to do so as worship honoring HaShem.[183]

PAGAN FESTIVALS

For the apostles, the larger concern was not whether to coerce the Gentiles to keep the Torah's appointed times, but whether or not the Gentiles had ceased participating in their former pagan practices, which included idolatrous festivals and holidays. As we read earlier, one of the four prohibitions placed on the Gentiles was to "abstain from what has been sacrificed to idols" (Acts 15:29), which in essence included all forms of pagan practice. Paul instructs the Gentile Corinthians to "flee from idolatry [*avodah zarah*]."[184]

Life outside of first-century Judaism was rooted in idolatry. Many Gentile believers probably found breaking completely with idolatry to be a major hurdle. Their new faith required them to remove themselves from everything with which they had been familiar.

Paul explicitly prohibits participation in pagan festivals in his letter to the Galatians:

> Formerly, when you did not know God, you were enslaved to those that by nature are not gods. But now that you have come to know God, or rather to be known by God, how can you turn back again to the weak and worthless elementary principles of the world, whose slaves you want to be once more? You observe days and months and seasons and years! (Galatians 4:8–10)

While some commentaries are tempted to interpret Galatians 4:8–10 as referring to the Jewish festivals, that interpretation raises difficulties. For example, Paul was writing to Gentiles who were formerly pagans.[185] Mark Nanos writes:

> This interpretation of Paul's reference to pagan timekeeping schemes related to the observation of local and imperial cults makes sense of the fact that Paul has identified the addressees as former idolaters in this context, not former righteous Gentiles or Jews.[186]

If the Galatian Gentiles were returning to anything, it would have been pagan celebrations which they had recently left and not to Jewish festivals with which they had no previous familiarity. Why would they want to return to former pagan ways? Nanos points out that because these Gentiles were not proselytes or candidates for conversion, they would not have been "protected from their pagan civic responsibilities by the authority of Jewish communal identity."[187] Therefore they would have had to face consequences, often harsh, for not participating in these required pagan festivities. More than just the practice of a religion, participation in the pagan holy days was their civic duty to the state. Rather than suffer for the cross, the Galatians were tempted either to convert, taking on the legally protected status of Jews, or to simply fulfill their duty by going through the motions of the pagan rituals.

In the absence of any of their former holidays and special occasions, Gentile believers would naturally want to participate with the rest of Israel in the festivals of the Torah. As with Shabbat, absence of any festivals or holy days would have created a serious spiritual vacuum.[188] If they did not celebrate the feasts of the Torah, what would they celebrate? Gentiles in Messiah had been "brought near" to the covenants and promises of Israel which included its festival calendar.[189] A natural outcome of that inclusion was to want to take on, at some level, the observance of the Jewish festivals. As is evident in the book of Acts, these Gentile believers attended synagogue and were consequently celebrating the holy days in some form simply by their attendance at services. We find evidence of this participation throughout the New Testament as well as in church history. A few examples will suffice for Passover, Shavuot, Yom Kippur, and Sukkot.

PASSOVER

Paul wrote the book of 1 Corinthians to a predominately Gentile audience who attended both synagogue and weekly gatherings of believers. Additionally, the timing of the letter seems to have been sometime in early spring before the Passover season had begun. Many portions in the letter give allusions to Passover and seem to be instructions for observing it properly with the right heart attitude.

> Your boasting is not good. Do you not know that a little leaven leavens the whole lump? Cleanse out the old

leaven that you may be a new lump, as you really are unleavened. For Christ, our Passover lamb, has been sacrificed. Let us therefore celebrate the festival, not with the old leaven, the leaven of malice and evil, but with the unleavened bread of sincerity and truth. (1 Corinthians 5:6–8)

Although the imagery to "celebrate the festival" is clearly metaphorical, it could really only be understood by those who were in fact literally celebrating Passover and the Festival of Unleavened Bread, complete with some level of abstention from leaven. Brian Rosner argues that this passage must be read in concert with 1 Corinthians 3:17: "For God's temple is holy, and you are that temple":

Having "cleansed the temple," Paul calls upon the congregation to celebrate spiritually the Festival of Passover/ Unleavened Bread in 1 Corinthians 5:7–8. That this sequence of events occurred to Paul's mind may itself testify to the influence of the Old Testament temple motif, since, in the Old Testament, there is an observable link between cleansing or restoring the temple and celebrating the Passover. Following the "removal of all defilement from the sanctuary" (2 Chron 29:5) in order to "reestablish the service of the temple of the LORD" (2 Chron 29:35), King Hezekiah in 2 Chronicles 30 calls upon the people to celebrate the Passover. Similarly, King Josiah, after removing the articles of idolatry from the temple and replacing the sacred ark in its rightful place, ordered the Israelites to celebrate the Passover and observe the Feast of Unleavened Bread (2 Chron 35:1–19; 2 Kings 23:1–23). Ezra followed the same pattern; Ezra 6 records first the completion and dedication of the temple (6:13–18) and then a joyous Passover and Feast of Unleavened Bread (6:19–22). It is intriguing that, even in the Gospels (Matt 21:12–13; Mark 11:15–18; Luke 19:45–47; John 2:13–22), as in 1 Corinthians 5, cleansing the temple and celebrating the Passover are connected.[190]

Thus cleansing the Temple from idolatry is often connected with the literal celebration of Passover. Apparently, the Gentile believers in Corinth were celebrating Passover in remembrance of Messiah.

David Rudolph writes of the widespread practice of Gentile believers celebrating Passover in the second century:

> It appears that almost all of the churches in Asia (where Paul devoted much of his ministry), as well as churches in Asia Minor, Cilicia, Syria, and Mesopotamia, observed Gentile Passover in accordance with the Jewish festival calendar, on the fourteenth day of the first month, the month of Nissan. Far from being a minor schismatic group, Christians who celebrated Gentile Passover on Nissan 14 stretched across a vast geographic region. Many of these Gentile Christians celebrated with Jews, and the similarity of their observance to Jewish Passover probably varied from community to community.[191]

When the Roman church sought to limit the celebration of Passover to the first Sunday after Passover, other Christians, especially those in Asia Minor, insisted on celebrating the festival according to the Jewish practice on the 14th of Nisan as they had always done. The venerable Bishop Polycarp, a disciple of the Apostle John, insisted that the Jewish observance of Passover had been transmitted to them through the apostles.[192] As the church at large began to adopt the Sunday practice instead, the Quartodecimans ("fourteeners," those who observed the fourteenth of Nissan) separated into their own sect. They existed up until the fifth century.

In the *Syriac Lectionary* (fifth century CE), the week before Easter is called the Week of Unleavened Bread.[193] The *Canons of Hippolytus* (third to fifth century CE) instructs:

> The week during which the Jews celebrated Passover must be observed by the Christian people with the greatest earnest, they must be careful to abstain from all eagerness.[194]

Although this text is not advocating Passover observance in the Torah sense per se, it does indicate that the early church retained traditions based upon Passover observances found in the Torah.

It indicates that, at some earlier point, the church was indeed observing the actual Jewish feast.

Rabbinic literature made room for non-Jews in Passover celebrations. In the Second-Temple era, Gentiles were not permitted to eat the actual Pesach sacrifice (Exodus 12:48), but they were allowed to eat unleavened bread and bitter herbs and participate in the rest of the seder meal.[195] It is likely that this is the practice the apostles would have followed as well with Gentiles celebrating Passover in Jerusalem.

SHAVUOT

The New Testament highlights the festival of Shavuot as the time of the outpouring of God's Spirit in Acts 2, but another reference in Acts 20 gives us some more evidence of Gentile believers celebrating the Torah's festivals:

> For Paul had decided to sail past Ephesus, so that he might not have to spend time in Asia, for he was hastening to be at Jerusalem, if possible, on the day of Pentecost. (Acts 20:16)

Paul wanted to make it to Jerusalem for Pentecost because Torah required all male Israelites to make a pilgrimage to the Temple on Shavuot.[196] While this gives clear evidence that Paul himself observed Shavuot, we can further speculate that this is evidence that Luke, the writer of Acts, did as well. Luke probably was a Gentile.[197] Luke's readers were "Christian God fearers," i.e., Gentile believers in Yeshua.[198] It seems unlikely that Luke would mention their trip to Jerusalem for Shavuot if the observance of that festival meant nothing to him or to his readers. The same could be said for Paul's statement in 1 Corinthians 16:8: "But I will stay in Ephesus until Pentecost." As we noted above, the letter to the Corinthians was written to a mixed community of Jews and Gentiles.

Additionally, from the context in Acts 20:16, we see that Paul brought Gentile believers with him to Jerusalem for the festival of Shavuot. For example, it is during this time that he was accused of bringing uncircumcised Greeks into the Temple because of his being seen with Trophimus the Ephesian in the city.[199] By bringing

Gentiles with him to Jerusalem for Shavuot, Paul was encouraging them to celebrate the holy day in the holy city.

Church history contains abundant testimony to the celebration of Shavuot, even down to the present day. One of the earliest references is found in the apocryphal book *Acts of Paul* (second century CE):

> While in prison, the brethren, since it was Pentecost, neither wept nor did they bow the knee, but they stood and prayed.[200]

Irenaeus also mentions Pentecost as a special day equal in holiness to the Lord's Day;[201] while Tertullian records it as one of the most joyful times.[202] Certainly Christian observance of the day varied from the customs of Judaism, but it is obvious that the Christian practice evolved from the celebration of the Feast of Weeks along with greater Judaism.

HIGH HOLY DAYS

Yom Kippur is to Judaism as Christmas is to Christianity; just as many Christians go to church on Christmas even if they never enter a church through the rest of the year, so too most Jews fast on Yom Kippur and attend synagogue services. It is a cultural and spiritual landmark. Not surprising then, we find a passing reference to this fast in the book of Acts:

> Since much time had passed, and the voyage was now dangerous because even the Fast was already over, Paul advised them, saying, "Sirs, I perceive that the voyage will be with injury and much loss, not only of the cargo and the ship, but also of our lives." (Acts 27:9–10)

"The Fast" referenced here is Yom Kippur. Stökl Ben Ezra assumes that Luke would not have used the term "the fast" as a calendaric reference unless he himself was keeping the fast and assumed that his readers were as well:

> I cannot help but draw the conclusion that Luke himself and his implied readers observed Yom Kippur. Why

else would Luke use a "Jewish calendaric reference for a secular problem?" He clearly presumes that his readers will understand what he is referring to.[203]

Scholars speculate that the readers of Acts were Gentiles like Luke himself. In order for Luke's readers to understand such a passing reference, they must have been observing Yom Kippur. Indirect evidence can be found in the book of Revelation. The book of Revelation is packed with allusions to the rituals and themes of the high holidays. The apocalyptic imagery—the day of judgment, the books of judgment, the blast of trumpets, the Temple scenes, and so forth—are all borrowed directly from the traditional observance of Rosh Hashanah and Yom Kippur. John addressed the book of Revelation to seven communities in Asia Minor, constituted predominantly by Gentiles. If those communities were not celebrating the high holidays along with the Jewish community, they would have been just as ill-prepared to decipher the book of Revelation as the church is today. Records of Gentile believers celebrating Yom Kippur appear in later church literature. The late second-century *Epistle to Diognetus* rails against Christians who observe Jewish laws such as "the Fast."[204] Origen mentions Christians fasting on Yom Kippur:

> Whence also we must say something now to those who think that in virtue of the commandments of the Law they must practice the fast of the Jews. (*Homily on Leviticus* 12:2 [Barkley])

He mentions another case, again involving Caesarean Christians, in his *Homilies on Jeremiah,* proving that this is not an isolated instance; there must have been at least several groups of Gentile Christians in the third century still celebrating this major fast day of Judaism.[205] In the late fourth century, John Chrysostom is still denouncing those who "join the Jews in keeping their festivals and observing their fasts."[206]

Further witness to this phenomenon can be found in the fifth-century medieval church practice of the Fast of the Seventh Month. This fast formed part of the Ember Days and was one of the most solemn days of the church's liturgical year. Scholars see this fast as the result of the Christianization of Yom Kippur.[207] In other words, because many Christian Gentiles were celebrating Yom Kippur, as the church began to split it from Judaism, Christianity slowly transformed it into a solely Christian fast in the month of September. This is similar to the transformation of Passover into Easter. The fifth-century theologian and pope Leo the Great wrote:

> We proclaim the holy Fast of the Seventh Month, dearly-beloved, for the exercise of common devotions, confidently inciting you with fatherly exhortations to make Christian by your observance that which was formally Jewish. (Sermon 90:1)

In this we once again see that many Gentile believers celebrated Yom Kippur, so much so that it remained even after the parting of the ways began to take place between Judaism and Christianity.

SUKKOT

Gentile observance of Sukkot is simply assumed in the book of Revelation. Chapter seven describes a scene where all nations are appearing before Messiah:

> After this I looked, and behold, a great multitude that no one could number, from every nation, from all tribes and peoples and languages, standing before the throne and before the Lamb, clothed in white robes, with palm branches in their hands, and crying out with a loud voice, "Salvation belongs to our God who sits on the throne, and to the Lamb!" … Therefore they are before the throne of God, and serve him day and night in his temple; and he who sits on the throne will shelter them with his presence. (Revelation 7:9–10, 15)

This motif clearly evokes the prophetic utterances of Zechariah in which everyone from the nations will come up to Jerusalem "to keep the Feast of Booths."[208] Here in Revelation, the nations come up to the throne of God in the Temple with palm branches in their hands which are the *lulav* (לולב) that the Torah commands to be waved on Sukkot.[209] *Midrash Tehillim* teaches that when the Messiah comes he will instruct the nations in the commandments of sukkah and *lulav* and indeed Rashi even feels, based on Zechariah 14, that these commandments will be incumbent upon them in the Messianic Era.[210] In Revelation 7:17 we find mention of "springs of living water," which appears to be a veiled reference to the water-pouring ceremony that took place in the Temple each morning of Sukkot,[211] thus reflecting major imagery of Sukkot.[212]

The Sukkot imagery in Revelation is intelligible only if it were written to a community of believers that was actually participating in the festivals of Israel. The communities reading Revelation were most assuredly made up of both Jewish and Gentile believers who celebrated Sukkot with the anticipation that the entire world would do so in the Messianic Age. Gentiles in Messiah celebrating it now are the firstfruits of that glorious time. Some scholars also see a connection between Sukkot and the later Feast of Encaenia ("Church Dedication"), both of which took place in the same season, lasted eight days, and were a time of pilgrimage to Jerusalem (with Sukkot to the Temple and with Encaenia to the Church of the Holy Sepulchre). Goudoever writes that "from the fourth century on, the Feast of Dedication is kept as a continuation of the third great Israelite feast [i.e., Sukkot].[213] There also appears to be a clear reference to Gentiles observing Sukkot in John Chrysostom's rebuke of those who, along with the Jews, had "tents … pitched among them."[214]

APPOINTED TIMES FOR ALL

Early church historian Jean Danielou points out that the earliest Christian documents contained no reference to a new liturgical calendar or list of holidays. Instead Jewish and Gentile believers kept the Torah's appointed times as their holy days:

> The Jewish liturgical year did clearly hold an important place in their eyes. The New Testament records the life of Christ in the setting of the Jewish feasts, and the importance attributed to this setting leads one to suppose that it still had some meaning for the communities to which the Gospels were addressed.[215]

From the evidence, it appears that the early believers, both Jew and Gentile, were celebrating the holy days of Israel. Although

Gentile believers were not to be judged regarding the festivals of the Torah, there is every reason to believe that in the early believing community, Gentile participation in the festivals and holy days was widespread. Unlike today, Judaism was the only game in town, and if Gentile believers chose not to celebrate these God-appointed holidays along with the rest of Israel, they would have been left with no special days of remembrance or joy.[216] Instead, we see evidence in the New Testament that Gentile believers celebrated the holy days along with the rest of Judaism. Early church literature provides evidence that many continued to do so even long after the majority of the church had rejected Torah observance. For Messianic Gentiles today, the early believing community is an example and source of encouragement. The first-century Gentile believers participated in the biblical feasts out of a love for the God of Israel, his only son Yeshua, and a desire to join in fully with the people of Israel on God's appointed times.

So far, we have made the case for a God-fearing Gentile believer's participation in the "signs" of the weekly and annual holy days of Israel, but we have not addressed the daily "sign" rituals of the Jewish people. How should the God-fearing Gentile believer relate to things like fringes on the corners of the garment, the wearing of tefillin, and placing a mezuzah on the doorpost?

CHAPTER SEVEN

TEFILLIN, TZITZIT, AND MEZUZAH

R. Eliezer b. Jacob said, "Whosoever has the tefillin on his head, the tefillin on his arm, the zizith on his garment, and the mezuzah on his doorpost, is in absolute security against sinning, for it is written, 'And a threefold cord is not quickly broken' (Ecclesiastes 4:12)." (b.*Menachot* 43b)

Now that we have discussed the relationship of Gentile believers to circumcision, Shabbat, and the festivals, we will examine the remaining sign commandments of tefillin, tzitzit, and mezuzah and their application (or lack thereof) to non-Jewish believers. In this chapter, I will present a quick overview of these three unique commandments. Those looking for a more in-depth treatment of the subjects should consult my short booklets: *Mezuzah, Tefillin,* and *Tzitzit.* All three are available through First Fruits of Zion as part of the Mayim Chayim series.

Let's start by looking at traditional Judaism's approach to the question. We will discuss the technical, legal, and rabbinic argumentation in Appendix 1, but for now, we need to take a cursory glance at how the sages of Israel felt about non-Jews observing these three commandments.

IN THE HALACHAH

Tefillin: Neither in the Talmud nor in any of the early rabbinic works do we find a prohibition against Gentiles wearing tefillin. There is a passage in the *Tosefta* that instructs Jews not to sell tefillin to Gentiles, and as some scholars point out, this may actually indicate that tefillin were worn by some non-Jews in that period.[217] Rabban Gamaliel's Gentile slave Tobi wore tefillin.[218] Even the later rabbinic codifier Rambam does not list tefillin as prohibited to Gentiles in his *Mishneh Torah*. However, all authorities including the Rambam agree that, if a Gentile does a commandment that he is not obligated to perform, he should do so without reciting the *brachah* "who has commanded us."[219] We also read in *Midrash Tehillim* that when the Messiah comes, he will teach the nations to observe thirty Torah commandants, including binding on tefillin.[220] Most halachic authorities today, however, frown upon Gentiles wearing tefillin.

Tzitzit: Early rabbinic literature poses no restrictions on Gentiles wearing tzitzit. There are some regulations about buying tzitzit from Gentiles and, like tefillin, it was forbidden to sell tzitzit to Gentiles.[221] The Rambam states if non-Jewish servants to Jews choose to observe the commandment of tzitzit, they are permitted to do so but without reciting the blessing, which says, "who has commanded us concerning tzitzit."[222] Yet, despite all this, as with tefillin, most modern rabbinic authorities discourage Gentiles from wearing tzitzit.[223]

Mezuzah: Neither early rabbinic literature nor the Rambam prohibit Gentiles from affixing a mezuzah, but is generally not considered permissible in the minds of most modern Jewish legal authorities. We do find a story in the *Jersualem Talmud* where Rabbi Yehudah HaNasi sends a mezuzah to the Persian King Artaban as a gift, which we can assume Artaban would put up.[224] There is also an injunction in the Talmud that a Jew may not leave a mezuzah on his house when he moves out if a Gentile is moving in, presumably because he will desecrate it.[225] If a legal authority did see it as permissible, he would no doubt agree that, like with tefillin and tzitzit, the *brachah* should not be recited by a Gentile when he affixes the mezuzah.

Judaism considers all three of these commandments as major demarcations between Jews and Gentiles. Many feel that, when non-Jews observe these commandments, they blur the line of distinction between Jewish and Gentile identity. Primarily for that reason, most modern-day rabbis and even Messianic Jewish rabbis discourage Gentiles from adopting these practices. Therefore, non-Jews need to be sensitive to Jewish sentiment and propriety as they consider the idea of embracing these distinctive markers of Jewish identity.

THE APOSTLES

Now that we have laid some groundwork from Judaism's perspective, let's examine the New Testament. It goes without saying that the apostles viewed all of the sign commandments as fully obligatory upon Jewish believers. Based upon Acts 15 and Paul's letters, we know that the apostles never bound the Gentile believers to these three commandments. At the same time, they did not directly address whether or not it was acceptable in their eyes for Gentiles to voluntarily embrace these outward signs of Jewish practice. However, in his first letter to the Corinthians, Paul off-handedly addresses the sign commandments as "the marks of circumcision," i.e., "Jewishness." Paul states this as his rule in all churches:

> Was anyone at the time of his call already circumcised? Let him not seek to remove the marks of circumcision. Was anyone at the time of his call uncircumcised? Let him not seek circumcision. (1 Corinthians 7:18)

One could interpret the phrase here, "marks of circumcision," as not just referring to conversion but also to the sign commandments in general. In other words, Jews who become believers should remain Torah-faithful, which includes observing the distinction of the sign commandments, but Gentiles should neither seek conversion nor try to look Jewish.

This seems in line with the rest of Paul's writings where he treads a fine line between balancing Jewish and Gentile oneness in Messiah while at the same time stressing distinctions and the unique callings for each group. Commenting on Paul's words "neither Jew nor Greek" (Galatians 3:28), D. Thomas Lancaster writes:

> In Messiah, Jew and Gentile are one but not the same. As regards salvation and our standing in the Messiah, there is no difference between Jew and Gentile. As the Apostle Peter declared, "He made no distinction between us and them, having cleansed their hearts by faith" (Acts 15:9). Jews, Gentiles, men, women, slaves, and freemen have the same access to salvation through the same Messiah, but that does not eliminate our distinct identities and roles.[226]

The biggest issue with Gentiles adopting external identity markers such as tefillin, tzitzit, and mezuzah is that they will appear Jewish and thus erode the uniqueness of the Jewish people. At the same time, their appearance sends a false message to the outside observer. They appear to be Jewish.

At first glance then, it seems that the apostles and the rabbinic authorities have the same concerns. But Gentile believers have been grafted in to the nation and are now, spiritually, a part of the commonwealth of Israel. As we have stated previously, this status may put them into a different category than the Gentiles outside of Messiah to whom the rabbis are directing their halachic rulings. Needless to say, the rabbinic world does not acknowledge Gentile faith in Yeshua as a factor in their decisions.

DISTINCTION AND RESPECT

Does this all mean that Gentiles should avoid wrapping tefillin, wearing tzitzit, and putting up a mezuzah on their house? Not necessarily. Each of these practices is deeply spiritual and can certainly enhance the Gentile disciple's walk in Messiah. All three commandments are intended to help one remember all the commandments of the Torah and to help keep the word of God near and dear to one's heart. The key to embracing them in healthy manner is to always keep the distinction of Jew and Gentile in mind.

For example, putting up a mezuzah on your doorpost when you live in a rural or backwoods area really doesn't pose an issue of blurring the lines of distinction. Instead, it can often spark the curiosity of visitors and be a great discussion starter. If, however, you live near or in a Jewish community in a major metropolitan area, it can make it appear to other Gentiles and Jews that you are Jewish. In cases like these, it might be better to place the mezuzah on the inner side of the doorpost of one's house so it is not visible from the street. This way one can participate in the mitzvah but not blur the lines of distinction and thus respect Jewish sensitivities.

The same type of principle can be applied to both tefillin and tzitzit. A Gentile believer who desires to wear tzitzit throughout the day would be well served to tuck them in so they are out of sight and not attracting attention. It also might be best to reserve the use of a tallit and tefillin for the privacy of his personal prayer time. Wearing these visibly can be like false advertising, and it communicates disrespect for the Jewish people. It looks to Jews like deception, and to non-Jewish believers it looks something like kids playing cowboy—dressing up Jewish.

Additionally, the tefillin, tzitzit, and mezuzah are reminders to obey the commandments of the Torah. Therefore, it would behoove a non-Jewish believer to actually know the command-ments that apply to him as a Gentile along with all their implica-tions before wearing or putting up something that is supposed to remind him of them. Too often, these outward signs become the first commandments that Gentiles attracted to Hebrew roots and Messianic Judaism decide to take on. They can quickly become a way to show off what one is learning to other believers. Just as our Master instructed in Matthew 23:5, we must never turn the fulfill-ment of commandments into pretentiousness.

Lastly, if a Gentile decides to take on the practice of tefillin, tzitzit, and mezuzah they should all be done in the traditional manner, with sensitivity to the rulings of the rabbis. Judaism has preserved rich and beautiful traditions. Gentile believers would be foolish to try and reinvent the wheel. Rather, we should honor the family into which we have been adopted.

A God-fearing Gentile believer who wishes to bind tefillin, wear tzitzit, and put up a mezuzah can regard these rituals as a wonderful sign of his adoption into the commonwealth of Israel and a beautiful connection with Messiah—an act of imitation of the Master. But it also can quickly become a stumbling block for the Jewish world and something that brings identity confusion to the Gentile believer. One must approach these areas slowly and carefully. On the other hand, when God-fearing Gentile believers observe these three commandments in a manner that is sensitive to greater Judaism and preserves distinction, they can be beautiful reminders of their connection to the Jewish people and the scriptures of Israel through Messiah. One must also continually bear in mind that, while non-Jewish believers are free to embrace these injunctions, they are not any less in the eyes of God if they choose not to do so.

CONCLUSION

Thus says the LORD of hosts: In those days ten men from the nations of every tongue shall take hold of the robe of a Jew, saying, "Let us go with you, for we have heard that God is with you." (Zechariah 8:23)

Who are the Gentiles practicing Messianic Judaism? We are the God-fearers. We non-Jews in Messiah who are seeking a proper relationship to the Jewish people and the Torah are resurrecting this ancient identity. Make no mistake, though. The theology of the apostles was that Gentiles in Messiah are grafted into Israel and have a place at the table with Abraham, Isaac, and Jacob. While distinction between Jew and God-fearing Gentile still remains, even in Messiah, we believing Gentiles are much more than just first-century God-fearers or even modern Noachides. We are not just resurrecting the title; in light of Messiah, we are redefining it as well.

Just as we have an eye on the past, we also have an eye on the future. The prophet Micah tells us that in the Messianic Era, "out of Zion shall go forth the Torah, and the word of the LORD from Jerusalem" (4:2). Isaiah prophesies that in that day all nations shall go up to Jerusalem, worship in the Temple, and offer sacrifices upon the altar (56:7). Zechariah states that men from all the nations will flock to the Jewish people and beg them to teach them the ways of Torah (8:23). By returning to the past, we are preparing for that future day. By starting to apply Torah to our lives now, we can begin to taste the Messianic kingdom.

This is not an easy path. It takes humility to be a God-fearing Gentile believer. We must recognize and respect the distinctions that exist in the Scriptures and honor the standing and calling of the Jewish people. For too long, we Gentile believers have minimized the importance of the Jewish people. Gentile believers might be grafted into the commonwealth of Israel and participants in God's plan for Israel, but we have not replaced the Jewish people. By returning to the path of the God-fearers, we should be restoring our respect and honor for the Jewish people. The Jewish people not only need our support, but they need us to guard their unique calling as God's chosen people.

God-fearers must also be champions of grace and kindness. The farther one gets down this path of restoration and reformation, the more one realizes how far the body of Messiah has strayed from its origin in first-century Messianic Judaism. This is one of those slippery slopes. If one is not careful, the Messianic life can quickly turn into criticism for the church and other brothers and sisters in Messiah who do not see things the same way. Leo Tolstoy once said, "Everyone wants to change the world, but nobody wants to change himself." God-fearers have a lot of work ahead of them to restore the ancient paths, but it begins with working on one's own heart and life. It does little good to rail against the errors of doctrines and theologies; we must walk the walk, and this includes patience and grace for those of our brothers and sisters within the mainstream church. As we all journey together toward the Messianic Era, we need to make room for all, regardless of where they are on the journey.

In this book we have covered quite a range of topics pertaining to non-Jewish participation in Messianic Judaism and the Torah life. It is a lot to process. For some, the discussion might be brand new and could feel overwhelming. For others, it might pose some challenges to what you believe. Wherever you are coming from, I encourage you to proceed slowly and cautiously, and don't just take my word for it; study it for yourselves.

I hope this study on God-fearers, both ancient and modern, has opened up fresh perspectives and encouraged my fellow Messianic Gentiles to reconsider what it means to be a Gentile disciple of Yeshua. I believe that the path of the Messianic God-fearing Gentile is a worthy path, one that represents a return to the authentic, historical lifestyle and mode of worship practiced by the first-century

Gentile believers, and connects them to the people of Israel. May HaShem give us all the strength to press on toward the goal!

> But grow in the grace and knowledge of our Master and Savior Yeshua the Messiah. To him be the glory both now and to the day of eternity. Amen. (2 Peter 3:18)

APPENDIX ONE

GENTILES OBSERVING TORAH IN JEWISH LAW

In discussing a Gentile's relationship to Torah, an inquiry into what the Jewish sages throughout the centuries have to say about non-Jews keeping the commandments is essential. While the Master and the apostles are the final authority for believers in Messiah on these materials, this inquiry will especially prove fruitful when it comes to being sensitive to the concerns of our Jewish brothers and sisters, both in Messianic Judaism and in mainstream forms of Judaism.

In modern Orthodox Judaism, the minimum standard of righteousness for Gentiles is the "seven laws of Noah," also known as the Noachide laws. Judaism regards these seven injunctions as the basis for godly living for those non-Jews among the nations who wish to join themselves in the worship of the God of Israel. Yet naturally the question arises as to how much of the Torah rabbinic halachah permits Gentiles to participate in beyond these seven laws. We will discover that the answer is not always cut and dried.

TECHNICAL TERMS FOR GENTILES

To begin with, we will need to define some terms as they are understood within conventional Judaism. There are three main classifications for Gentiles who have joined themselves to Judaism. The first is a *ger tzedek* ("proselyte," גר צדק), which is a Gentile who has undergone full conversion to Judaism and is considered by Jewish law to be a Jew in every respect.[227]

The second is a *ger toshav* ("resident stranger," גר תושב). This is a Gentile who lived among ancient Israel in their nation and was under legal protections by Israel, which included receiving charity if necessary. According to the Talmud, they were required to make a formal proclamation renouncing idolatry before a Jewish court of law (*beit din*, בית דון) and then, according to one opinion, to keep all of the commandments of the Torah with the exception of the prohibition to eat a *nevelah* (נבלה), i.e., an animal that has died of itself.[228] Maimonides states that the *ger toshav* is merely obligated to obey the seven laws of Noah.[229] While this category is at times difficult to define precisely according to halachah, this classification of Gentiles is not applicable today when the Jubilee year is not being observed.[230] Therefore there is not a category of the "resident stranger" in Judaism currently. Nevertheless, the *ger toshav* category most closely conforms to the status of the God-fearing Gentiles of the first-century synagogue world.

The last category is that of a *benei Noach* ("sons of Noah," בני נח). According to Judaism, all non-Jews who have not converted are of this status today. They are therefore bound to the seven laws of Noah. It is this last category—the Noachides—that we will deal with primarily, because rabbinic literature addresses this category directly.

In traditional Jewish law, a *ben Noach* (son of Noah, i.e., a Gentile) is bound to seven universal laws: the prohibitions of blasphemy, idolatry, adultery, murder, robbery, eating flesh from a living animal, and the requirement to set up law courts.[231] The codification of these laws seems to have taken place over hundreds of years, and they began to take solid shape in the Talmud during the Amoraic period (200–500 CE).[232] Yet we also find discussion in rabbinic literature of additional laws for which Gentiles might be responsible, such as the prohibitions against sorcery, emasculation, and mixing seed, and the positive injunctions of procreation and respecting the Torah.[233] In fact there is even a suggestion, based on Zechariah 11:13, that nations were obligated to a total of thirty commandments.[234] Nevertheless, today it is unanimously accepted within Orthodox Judaism that these seven are the minimum requirements for those Gentiles who wish to have a share in the world to come. Maimonides writes:

> Anyone who accepts upon himself the fulfillment of these seven mitzvot and is precise in their observance is considered one of "the pious among the nations" and will merit a share in the world to come. (*Mishneh Torah, Melachim* 8:11 [Touger])

So this now brings us back to our original question. According to Jewish law if Gentiles wish to do more than the seven laws of Noah but do not want to convert and become legally Jewish, how much of Torah does halachah permit them to do?

Noachide Gentiles are permitted to learn and grow in the Torah's instruction.[235] For example, although Gentiles are not specifically required to honor their father and mother, they are encouraged to do so, and the Talmud records numerous stories of a Gentile named Dama ben Nesina who is said to be unsurpassed in his observance of this precept.[236] Yet throughout history we do find some opinions limiting how much Torah a *ben Noach* can observe.

IN THE TALMUD

The Talmud was codified in about 400 CE. The Talmud forbids only the observance of two commandments: Torah study and Shabbat. This is important because the Talmud becomes the basis for all later halachic decisions. Here is what it says about Gentiles keeping Shabbat:

> Resh Lakish also said: "A heathen who keeps a day of rest, deserves death, for it is written, 'And a day and a night they shall not rest' (Genesis 8:22), and a master has said: 'Their prohibition is their death sentence.'" Rabina said: "Even if he rested on a Monday." (b.*Sanhedrin* 58b)[237]

While at first glance this seems very harsh to decree that if a Gentile observes Shabbat he deserves death, it was probably not meant literally but rather expresses the severity with which the Sages viewed this transgression.[238] We find similar language in the prohibition of a Gentile to study the Torah.

R. Johanan said: "A heathen who studies the Torah deserves death, for it is written, 'Moses commanded us a law for an inheritance' (Deuteronomy 33:4), it is our inheritance, not theirs ..." An objection is raised: "R. Meir used to say. 'Whence do we know that even a heathen who studies the Torah is as a High Priest? From the verse, "[Ye shall therefore keep my statutes, and my judgments:] which, if man do, he shall live in them" (Leviticus 18:5). Priests, Levites, and Israelites are not mentioned, but men: hence thou mayest learn that even a heathen who studies the Torah is as a High Priest!'"—That refers to their own seven laws. (b.*Sanhedrin* 59a)[239]

In this passage, a Gentile is only permitted to study the laws that are applicable to him, in particular the seven laws of Noah. Once again, the death penalty should not be seen as meant literally but rather serves as a strong warning.

As we pointed out in chapter five, an interesting suggestion has been made that these two passages did not originally refer to Gentiles but rather to Christians.[240] Talmudic manuscripts exist with a textual variant that contains the acronym *akkum* (עכו"ם), which means "astrologer" or "idolater" and not just Gentile. So these prohibitions may just have been a polemic against idolatry and/or Christianity and not a sweeping prohibition against Shabbat and Torah study for all non-Jews.

Although not explicitly forbidden, it does appear that the Talmudic-era sages frowned upon Gentiles wearing tzitzit:

> Our Rabbis taught: "If a man bought a garment furnished with tzitzit from an Israelite in the market, the presumption is [that it is valid]; if he bought it from a gentile, who was a merchant, it is valid, but if he was a private individual it is invalid." And [this is so] not withstanding that they said, "A man may not sell a garment furnished with tzizit to a gentile unless he removed the tzitzit." What is the reason for this?—Here it was explained, on account of a harlot. Rab Judah said, "It is to be feared that [an Israelite] might join him on the road and he might kill him." (b.*Menachot* 43a)

In the times of the Talmud anti-Semitism was rampant, and the sages felt it was wise to set up distances between themselves and their Gentile neighbors.

The Talmud says that Torah scrolls, mezuzot, and tefillin that were written by Gentiles are invalid.[241]

Besides finding only a few commandments Gentiles were forbidden to observe, we do see an example in the Jersualem Talmud where Rabbi Yehudah HaNasi sends a mezuzah to the Persian King Artaban as a gift.[242] Assumedly Artaban would put it up which, as will be noted, according to modern Jewish interpretation, is forbidden.[243] In fact in another place the Talmud instructs that a Jew may not leave a mezuzah on his house when he moves out if a Gentile is moving in, presumably because he will desecrate it.[244]

ACCORDING TO RAMBAM

In his *Mishneh Torah*, Rambam (1135–1204) sought to systematically lay out all the halachic rulings of the Talmud in an orderly code. The Rambam himself is considered one of the greatest sages and halachic scholars of all time, and his work is highly respected and cited frequently in Orthodox Judaism today.

In Rambam's *Mishneh Torah* we find the same two prohibitions on non-Jews that we find in the Talmud: those of Torah study and of Shabbat observance.

> A gentile who studies Torah is obligated to die. They should be involved only in their study of the seven mitzvot. Similarly, a gentile who rests, even on a weekday, observing that day as a Sabbath, is obligated to die. Needless to say, [he is obligated to punishment] if he creates a festival for himself … They may either become righteous converts and accept all the mitzvot or retain their statutes without adding or detracting from them. *(Mishneh Torah, Melachim* 10:9 [Touger])

Here he is following the standard line of the Talmud. He goes on to say that although he is deserving of death, he should not be executed.

Rambam also mentions, in a different section, the prohibition of selling a garment with tzitzit on it to a Gentile for the same reasons as the Talmud.[245] The situation for Jews was no better in his day than it was for the Sages in the Talmud, but once again, the ruling never explicitly states that Gentiles cannot wear tzitzit. Rambam also states that a Gentile may not make or write Torah scrolls, mezuzot, or tefillin.[246]

Perhaps the most remarkable comment he made was right after the section about the prohibitions of Shabbat and Torah study. He stated:

> We should not prevent a gentile who desires to perform one of the Torah's mitzvot in order to receive reward from doing so, [provided] he performs it as required. (*Mishneh Torah, Melachim* 10:10 [Touger])[247]

What he seems to imply here is that a Gentile may observe any commandment besides Shabbat and Torah study and will receive a blessing in doing so.[248] Thus, this statement from the Rambam is probably the strongest statement we have in rabbinic literature inviting Gentiles to participate in the Torah if they so desire. The *Chatam Sofer* points out that this is not in contradiction to what he said above in *Melachim* 10:9 and that he feels this even includes Shabbat and Torah study:

> See Rambam, Laws of Kings, chapter 10, halachah 9 and 10, where it appears that he distinguishes between an idol worshipper and a Ben Noach, who is one who has accepted upon himself not to be an idolater; and for such a person it is permitted to cease [from work on the Sabbath] and to fulfill any commandment that he desires; and from such a person they accept sacrificial offerings, teach him Torah, and accept charity from him.[249]

THE HALACHAH TODAY

Although we have not examined all the sources on the topic, both the Talmud and the *Mishneh Torah* provide the major basis for today's rulings on Torah observance for Gentiles. Today, the majority of halachic authorities are of the opinion that there are commandments which are forbidden unto Gentiles. These include:[250]

1. Tefillin (including wearing, making, or writing)
2. Mezuzah (writing or affixing on one's house)
3. Shabbat (observing it in a traditional manner)
4. Festivals (observing them in a traditional manner)
5. Torah Scroll (writing one or reading from one in a formal synagogue service)
6. Talmud Torah (studying sections of the Torah that do not apply to Gentiles)

The common reason given for the first three prohibitions is that as we have mentioned the Torah speaks of each of these three commandments as a sign (*ot*, אות).[251] For example, in Exodus 31:13 we read, "It is a sign (*ot*) forever between me and the people of Israel," which according to Rabbi Yehuda ben Yakar means that Shabbat is an inheritance for Jews only.[252] While some authorities forbid Gentiles from even resting from work on the seventh day, it is generally seen only as prohibited for a Gentile to observe Shabbat (and all Festivals) in a traditional manner.[253] According to this interpretation, tefillin, mezuzah, and Shabbat are specific signs that separate the children of Israel from the nations around them. Rav Moshe Feinstein writes:

> But regarding Sabbath and Yom Tov observance and laying tefillin, and wearing *tzitzit*, and *sukkah*, and *lulav*, and *shofar*, and eating kosher food, and not wearing *shatnez*, and all similar manners, a non-Jew would receive no reward for such observance, because non-Jews are excluded from these mitzvot, since they did not receive the Torah, and these are not considered mitzvot for them.[254]

The prohibitions on reading from the Torah in a service and studying the Torah are presumably based upon the Talmudic dictum that a Gentile should not be reading or studying parts of the Torah that do not apply to him. Rabbi Schwartz writes:

It is important to study the laws of the Torah that apply to Noahides. However they are prohibited from studying those parts of the Torah that don't apply to them. This refers mainly to the oral law (Talmud, Rambam etc.) but also when reading the Bible it is better to skip those laws that don't apply to them.[255]

Additionally, though not included in this list, Noachides are generally discouraged from wearing tzitzit, but it does not appear that they are not prohibited from doing so by halachah.

One notable exception to this is Rabbi Chaim Kanievsky, a world-renowned Israeli Haredi *posek* ("legal authority"). He has ruled that a Gentile who has taken upon himself the "seven laws of Noah" may then take upon himself any other mitzvah of Torah.[256] Although this opinion belongs to the minority, it is astounding to see such a view expressed by an Orthodox halachic authority.

Rabbi Michael Shelomo Bar-Ron continues in this same vain:

> For such people it is important to point out that the Seven Laws are a beginning—not an end. With only a few exceptions a Noahide may practice any of the Torah obligations of a Jew and receive a Heavenly reward. Therefore, those whose soul thirsts for more closeness to HaShem and to fulfill more of His Torah Commandments, there is tremendous room for growth beyond the Seven.[257]

He goes on to suggest that while a Gentile may observe commandments such as tzitzit, tefillin, and mezuzah, they should be done "in such a way that he will not be mistaken for a Jew, and be seen doing something forbidden to observant Jews."[258] He even makes room for Gentiles praying out of a traditional siddur and "imitating Jewish prayer in all its details."[259]

IN THE MESSIANIC AGE

Before we end our discussion on Torah observance for Gentiles in rabbinic law, we will turn our attention to an examination of the Messianic Age. In early rabbinic literature there seems to be a stream of thought that most Gentiles from among the nations would eventually turn to full or almost-full Torah observance. We read in the Midrash:

> R. Tanchuma said: The King Messiah will come for no other purpose than to teach the nations of the earth thirty precepts, such as those of the Booth, the Palm-Branch, and the Tefillin. But all the children of Israel will be taught the Torah by the Holy One Himself, blessed be He, for it is said All the children shall be taught by the Lord (Isa. 59:13). Why not by the Messiah? Because it is said Unto him shall the nations seek. (*Midrash Tehillim* 21 [Braude])[260]

Here it is believed that the Messiah will come and teach the nations to observe the Torah, including commandments like building a Sukkah, waving the *lulav,* and binding on tefillin. It is fascinating to see that here it is the Messiah who will teach the nations Torah. For believers, this brings to mind the words of our Master: "Go therefore and make disciples of all nations … teaching them to observe all that I have commanded you."[261] In the Jerusalem Talmud, we read that in the Messianic Era the Gentiles will take upon themselves the whole yoke of Torah:

> R. Hiyya bar Luliani in the name of R. Hoshaiah: "All of the commandments [not just thirty] are the children of Noah destined to accept upon themselves." (y.*Avodah Zarah* 2:1 [Neusner])

The Talmud further explains that this will include tzitzit and tefillin. The passage goes on to say that the nations will ultimately throw off the yoke of the Torah. Nevertheless, we see that the idea of Gentiles turning to Torah in the Messianic Age is found firmly within the earliest wells of rabbinic thought.[262]

The Rambam also picks up on this theme in his *Mishneh Torah*:

> If a king will arise from the House of David who diligently contemplates the Torah and observes its mitzvot … He will then improve the entire world, [motivating] all the nations to serve God together, as [Zephaniah 3:9] states: "I will transform the peoples to a purer language so that

they all will call upon the name of God and serve with one purpose." (*Mishneh Torah, Melachim* 11:4 [Touger])

He foresees that one of the signs of the Messiah is to lead the nations back to the worship of the one true God. This seems to indicate that the nations have not just accepted the Noachide laws but all of the Torah. Everyone—Jew and Gentile—will be worshipping HaShem together.

> In that era, there will be neither famine or war, envy or competition for good will flow in abundance and all delights will be freely available as dust. The occupation of the entire world will be solely to know God. (*Mishneh Torah, Melachim* 12:5 [Touger])

There are divided views as to what exactly this means. Some scholars are of the opinion that the Rambam envisions all the nations of the earth converting to Judaism.[263] This would seem to be in accordance with the Talmud.

> R. Simeon b. Eleazar says: "Outside Palestine also one should say this, because they will one day become proselytes, as it says, 'For then will I turn to the peoples a pure language [Zephaniah 3:9].'" (b.*Brachot* 57b)

Others such as Ya'akov Blidstein are of the opinion that "according to Maimonides the distinction between Jew and Gentile will simply disappear during the time of the Messiah—in effect, there will be neither Jews nor Gentiles, only human beings who worship God in concert."[264] At the very least, these passages of the Rambam also support the idea of Gentiles turning to the Torah in the Messianic Era.

CONCLUSION

We have only taken a cursory look at the rabbinic literature that deals with this subject. There are many more intricacies and details that we have left undiscussed. Nonetheless, even this short review of the relevant literature reveals that the idea of Gentiles keeping Torah is not as foreign to Judaism as one might think.

Although modern Jewish halachah regards Gentiles keeping Torah (especially a few of the more overt signs of Torah observance) as taboo, earlier rabbinic literature indicates that these opinions have evolved over time. It seems that the rise of Christianity, of Christian anti-Semitism, and of hostility to Judaism in general, led the sages towards halachic rulings that caused sharper and clearer distinctions between Jews and non-Jews—even for those non-Jews who would call themselves Noachides in an attempt to join with Judaism in worshipping the God of Israel.

As we stated at the outset, our purpose in this inquiry has not been to seek permission from the sages of Israel for Gentile Torah observance. One must remember that traditional Judaism lacks the revelation regarding Gentile believers that was given to us through the words of Yeshua and the ministry of his apostles. The rulings above reflect Jewish opinion regarding the *ben Noach*. God-fearing Gentile believers transcend that category. We are no longer strangers to the covenant of Israel, and we are servants of the King of the Jews. We are more akin to the *ger toshav*, that is the stranger who lived among the Jewish people within Jewish territory, than we are to the *ben Noach*.

Nevertheless, Jewish scholars have been studying and making rulings on the Torah for thousands of years. The Jewish people "were entrusted with the oracles of God." [265] The opinions of the rabbis should, at the very least, be an important point of reference for Gentile believers seeking to pursue a life of Torah. As witnesses for the Master, it is essential to show sensitivity towards the rulings of traditional Judaism.

GER AS PROSELYTE

BY AARON EBY AND TOBY JANICKI

The discussion of the biblical God-fearers requires a look at the Jewish convention of conversion to Judaism. A Gentile God-fearer is a Gentile monotheist who has taken on many of the practices of Judaism and yet has not undergone a legal conversion to become Jewish. Judaism distinguishes between two types of proselytes: the *ger tzedek* (a full proselyte) and the *ger toshav* (resident alien). The *ger tzedek* aquires legal Jewish identity by means of circumcision and a conversion ritual supervised by the Jewish community. The *ger tzedek* is obligated to the whole Torah as a Jew; indeed, he is considered Jewish after his conversion. The apostles treated the God-fearing Gentile believer not as *ger tzedek* but as a type of *ger toshav.*

The biblical Hebrew word *ger* means "stranger." By the end of the Second-Temple era in which the apostolic community lived, the semantic value of the word *ger* had shifted somewhat. In the "one-law" passages discussed in chapter two, we saw several verses which declared that there shall be "one law for the native among the sons of Israel and for the *ger.*"[266]

The predominant view in Judaism says that the term *ger* in those passages does not denote a resident alien non-Jew (*ger toshav*), but a full proselyte to Judaism (*ger tzedek*). This type of a *ger* was a person who had joined with the Jewish people and religion through a formal conversion process.

In the late Second Temple times, the term *ger* had become virtually synonymous with "proselyte," and strangers were admitted to the religious fellowship of Israel.[267]

Milgrom explains that the word *ger* had already taken on the meaning of proselyte three hundred years prior to the apostles.[268] Scholars find evidence of this semantic shift in a variety of ancient sources. The new semantic value of *ger* is fully developed, for example, in Philo (20 BCE –50 CE).[269] The Greek version of the Torah (Septuagint or LXX) frequently translates the word *ger* as "proselyte" (*proselutos*, προσηλυτος), but where context would render such an interpretation nonsensical, a more generic word for "foreigner" is used. Shaye Cohen explains:

> In those passages of the Torah that emphasize the social inequality of the resident alien, the Septuagint usually translates *ger* with *paroikos*, Greek for "resident alien;" in those passages in the Torah that emphasize the legal equality of the resident alien, the Septuagint usually translates *ger* with *proselutos*, a new Greek word.[270]

Proselutos literally means "newcomer," but by the time of the apostles, the Jewish community used the word *proselutos* to refer exclusively to a Gentile who had undergone a legal conversion to Judaism.

To the Jewish people in the days of the apostles, the "native" and "stranger" mentioned by the "one-law" passages did not mean Jew and Gentile. "Natives" meant people born Jewish; "strangers" meant converts to Judaism. But contrary to the historical, grammatical, contextual reading, the sages understood the term "one torah" as referring to the entire Torah, not just a single statute about sacrificial procedure:

> I might understand that the proselyte is like the born Jew only with respect to Passover. How about all the other commandments of the Torah? Scripture says: "One law shall be to him that is homeborn, and unto the stranger." This passage comes to declare the proselyte equal to the born Jew with respect to all the commandments of the Torah. (*Mekhilta* on Exodus 12:49 [JPS])

A LEGAL TRANSITION

Ancient literature shows that Second-Temple era Jews understood *ger* as a legal convert to Judaism. A convert to Judaism was considered to be under obligation to all the Torah's commandments in the same way as native-born Jewish people. They were even forbidden from marrying Gentiles.[271] In all respects, a convert became a Jew. But in what sense? How could a Gentile become Jewish?

A proselyte is a Gentile who goes through a legal conversion to become legally Jewish. That does not mean that a Gentile can become "ethnically" Jewish. One might be led to think so by later rabbinic texts such as those that describe a convert as "as Israel in every respect" (ישראל לכל דבריו),[272] or "like a child newly born" (כקטן שנולד),[273] a term that bears resonance with John 3. Despite texts such as these, neither Second-Temple era Judaism(s) nor later rabbinic Judaism considered the change that took place at conversion to be biological or "ethnic." Rather, the change from being a Gentile to being a Jew was considered a legal transition, and that is why it impacted obligation to Torah. This is apparent from the fact that conversion has a practical impact on one's observance, particularly in regards to family relationships.

The legal transition from Gentile to Jew can be compared to the legal status change that occurs when one adopts a child or gets married. No biological transformation occurs, but their status is affected in a very real and practical way in civil law.

The legal perspective is illustrated by the rabbinic requirement that a court of three (*beit din*) must preside over the conversion process. The sages derived the concept that conversion is a legal concern from the biblical text itself:

> Rabbi Chiya bar Abba said in the name of Rabbi Yochanan, "A convert [*ger*] requires three [judges, because the word] 'judgment' [*mishpat*] is written concerning him [in Numbers 15:16]." (b. *Yevamot* 46b)

In other words, it mattered *legally* whether someone was obligated or not. It had bearing, not just on their personal relationship with God but in legal matters in a Torah community.

We must remember that the Torah is not merely a personal guidebook to life, but in its original context it was given as a national constitution and foundation for civil law, to be arbitrated by judges in courts of justice. Many of the traditional Jewish interpretations of the Torah come from their experience applying it in this legal, national context.

In certain cases, it was absolutely necessary for a court of law to determine legally if a person was liable to certain laws or not. For example, suppose that a Gentile was found gathering sticks on the Sabbath and brought before the Sanhedrin. Should he be stoned?

To clarify such ambiguities, Second-Temple era Judaism taught that Gentiles who felt a calling to join the people of Israel and their God had the ability to do so by means of a conversion. As a legal process, this conversion was essentially a change of nationality or citizenship. One who converted was not biologically transformed into a member of the Jewish "race"; rather, he was naturalized into the Jewish nation. Like an immigrant to the United States who becomes naturalized as a citizen, he could enter into a contractual and constitutional legal agreement with the other people of the nation. Just as American civil law applies in special ways for citizens, granting them additional privileges (such as voting) and responsibilities (such as jury duty), so does the Torah apply in a special way for legally bound citizens of Israel.

The ritual of conversion cannot be dismissed simply because it is "man-made." It was based squarely on legal and covenantal norms found in the Torah, including the commandment of circumcision and the covenant initiation ceremonies in the Torah. Saying that it is "man-made" and therefore irrelevant would be a bit like saying that a marriage is illegitimate because the wedding ceremony was not explicitly written out in the Bible.

APOSTOLIC PERSPECTIVE ON CONVERTS

So far, we have shown that to the ancient Israelites, a *ger* may not have been considered an Israelite, but neither was he or she considered obligated to all of the Torah's commands. To the Jews who lived in the days of the apostles, a *ger tzedek* was considered obligated to the entire Torah, but they were also considered Jews, having gone through a legal process of conversion.

What matters most to us is how the apostolic community understood it. Did they see the Torah through the same lens as the Jewish communities from which they emerged?

On one hand, Paul spoke of believing Gentiles in terms of citizenship and even the covenants of Israel:

> Remember that you were at that time separated from Christ, alienated from the commonwealth of Israel and strangers to the covenants of promise, having no hope and without God in the world. But now in Christ Jesus you who once were far off have been brought near by the blood of Christ. (Ephesians 2:12–13)

On the other hand, Acts 15, Galatians, and Paul's other writings make it clear that they did not hold the Gentile believers to the proselyte standard of equal obligation to the Torah.

We do not have any indication that the apostles reinvented Judaism or objected to contemporary interpretations, seeking to restore a Moses-era interpretive model. They continued to practice the form of Second-Temple Judaism with which they were familiar. Therefore, the apostles would not have understood the one-law passages any differently than their Jewish contemporaries.

Several passages in the New Testament indicate that the apostles recognized the category of the proselyte (convert) to Judaism. The tie between apostolic thought and contemporary Judaism of their day is bolstered by the fact that *proselutos* is an invented Greek word that does not appear outside of Jewish and Christian texts.[274]

Luke acknowledges proselytes in the narratives of Acts. In Acts 2:11 he differentiates between "Jews and proselytes." In Acts 6:5 he mentions that one of the seven deacons was "a proselyte from Antioch." In Acts 13:43, he mentions "Jews and devout proselytes" who were intrigued by Paul's message. Paul himself differentiates between Jews, proselytes, and God-fearing Gentiles in Acts 13:26.[275]

It is well known that the Greek LXX text was commonly employed by the apostolic communities and considered to be an accepted standard. This gives us an indication of how the apostolic community would have understood and interpreted the "one-law" passages. We have already seen that the LXX often translated the word *ger* as "proselyte" (προσηλυτος). Under the influence of the LXX, they would have interpreted Numbers 15:15–16 to read as follows:

> As for the assembly, there shall be one statute for Jews and for the proselyte, a perpetual statute throughout your generations; as a Jew is, so shall the proselyte be before the LORD. There is to be one Torah and one ordinance for Jews and for the proselyte who sojourns with you. (Numbers 15:15–16; paraphrased)

If the apostles accepted this reading, then from their perspective, both Jews and proselytes to Judaism were obligated to the same laws of Torah and liable to a Torah court of law for the same punishments for violations of Torah.

The debate that frames Acts 15 hinges on the question of whether or not the Gentile believers should be considered as full proselytes (*ger tzedek*) or merely God-fearers among Israel (*ger toshav*).

Unless the apostles decided that the Gentile believers qualified as full proselytes (*ger tezdek*) with legal Jewish status, they could not have applied the Torah's "one-law" passages to them. The legal obligations of the conversion process are taken as a matter of fact in Paul's argument in Galatians 5:3: "I testify again to every man who accepts circumcision that he is obligated to keep the whole law." [276]

Although Paul discouraged people from undergoing conversion, he did not do so because he saw it as an invalid, man-made institution. Rather, he discouraged conversion because he believed it to increase an individual's obligation to certain commandments (an obligation that the proselyte might not be willing to meet) and because his theological opponents viewed it as a prerequisite for salvation. David Flusser believes the apostolic view of not requiring conversion for Gentiles is in line with the Master:

> The liberal school of Hillel was not distressed to see Gentiles becoming Jews. By contrast, the school of Shammai made conversion as difficult as possible. The following sayings show that Jesus shared the strict standpoint of Shammai. "Woe to you scribes and Pharisees, hypocrites! For you traverse sea and land to make a single proselyte,

and when he becomes a proselyte, you make him twice as much a child of hell as yourselves" (Matt. 23:15). A non-Jew who lives according to certain fundamental moral laws, without following the whole mosaic law, is blessed. The proselyte, the Gentile who has converted to Judaism, however, is bound by the whole law. If a proselyte fails to fulfill the whole law, which formerly did not obligate him, his conversion to Judaism is itself the cause of his becoming a child of hell. Quite needlessly he has thrown away his blessedness.[277]

In Messiah, Gentile believers are sons of Abraham and have been grafted into the olive tree of Israel. There is no need for Gentile believers to feel like second-class citizens or seek some further status or affirmation by pursuing conversion. The Apostle Paul strongly discourages Gentiles from doing so.

WORKS CITED

Adler, Cyrus, Gotthard Deutsch, Louis Ginzberg, Richard Gottheil, Joseph Jacobs, Marcus Jastrow, Morris Jastrow, Jr., Kaufmann Kohler, Frederick de Sola Mendes, Crawford H. Toy, and Isidore Singer, eds. *Jewish Encyclopedia.* 12 vols. New York, NY: Funk and Wagnalls, 1906.

Adler, Elchanan. "The Sabbath Observing Gentile: Halakhic, Hashkafic and Liturgical Responses." *Tradition* 36 no. 3 (2002): 14–45.

Attar, Rabbi Chayim ben. *Or HaChayim: Commentary on the Torah.* 5 vols. Translated by Eliyahu Munk. New York, NY: Lambda Publishers, 1999.

Bacchiocchi, Samuele. *From Sabbath to Sunday: A Historical Investigation of the Rise of Sunday Observance in Early Christianity.* Rome: The Pontifical Gregorian University Press, 1977.

Bamberger, Bernard J. *Proselytism in the Talmudic Period.* New York, NY: KTAV Publishing House, 1968.

Barkley, Gary Wayne. *Origen: Homilies on Leviticus 1-16.* Washington, DC: Catholic University of America Press, 1990.

Barnett, Paul. *The New International Commentary on the New Testament: The Second Epistle to the Corinthians.* Grand Rapids, MI: Eerdmans, 1997.

Bar-Ron, Rabbi Michael Shelomo. *Guide for the Noahide: A Complete Manual for Living by the Noahide Laws.* Springdale, AR: Lightcatcher Books, 2010).

Bauckham, Richard. *The Book of Acts in Its First Century Setting, Volume 4: Palestinian Setting.* Grand Rapids, MI: Eerdmans, 1995.

Ben Ezra, Daniel Stökl. "Christians Observing 'Jewish' Festivals of Autumn." Pages 53–73 in *The Image of Judaeo-Christians in Ancient Jewish and Christian Literature*. Edited by Peter J. Tomson and Doris Lambers-Petry. Tubingen, Germany: Moher Siebeck, 2003.

Ben Ezra, Daniel Stökl. "Whose Fast is It? The Ember Day of September and Yom Kippur," Pages 259–282 in *The Ways That Never Parted*. Edited by Adam H. Becker and Annette Yoshiko Reed. Tubingen, Germany: Moher Siebeck, 2003.

Bercot, David W. *A Dictionary of Early Christian Beliefs*. Peabody, MA: Hendrickson Publishers, 1998.

Boteach, Shmuley. *Judaism for Everyone: Renewing Your Life through Vibrant Lessons of the Jewish Faith*. New York, NY: Basic Books, 2002.

Botterweck, G. Johannes and Helmer Ringgren, eds. *Theological Dictionary of the Old Testament*. 11 vols. Translated by John T. Willis. Grand Rapids, MI: Eerdmans, 1997.

Braude, William G. *The Midrash to the Psalms*. 2 vols. Dexter, MI: Yale University, 1959.

Brown, F., S. Driver, and C. Briggs. *Brown-Driver-Briggs Hebrew and English Lexicon*. Peabody, MA: Hendrickson Publishers, 1999.

Chaniotis, Angelos. "Godfearers in the City of Love." *Biblical Archaeology Review* 36 no. 3 (May/June 2010): 32–44, 77.

Chavel, Charles B. *Maimonides: The Commandments Volume One: Positive*. New York, NY: Soncino Press, 1967.

Clorfene, Chaim and Ya'akov Rogalsky. *The Path of the Righteous Gentile*. Southfield, MI: Targum Press, 1987.

Cohen, Shaye J. D. *The Beginnings of Jewishness*. Berkeley, CA: University of California Press, 1998.

Cohn, Yehudah B. *Tangled Up in Text: Tefillin and the Ancient World*. Providence, RI: Brown Judaic Studies, 2008.

Cross, F. L. and E. A. Livingston, eds. *The Oxford Dictionary of the Christian Church*. 3rd ed. Oxford: Oxford University Press, 2005.

Danielou, Jean. *The Theology of Jewish Christianity*. Translated by John A. Baker. Philadelphia, PA: Darton, Longman and Todd, 1978.

Draper, Jonathan. "The Holy Vine of David Made Known to the Gentiles through God's Servant Jesus: 'Christian-Judaism' in the Didache." Pages 257–283 in *Jewish Christianity Reconsidered*. Edited by Jonathan Draper. Minneapolis, MN: Fortress Press, 2007.

Eby, Aaron. *Biblically Kosher: A Messianic Jewish Perspective on Kashrut*. Marshfield, MO: First Fruits of Zion, 2012.

Fahlbusch, Erwin, Jan Milic Lochman, John Mbiti, Jaroslav Pelikan, and Lukas Vischer, eds. The Encyclopedia of Christianity. 5 vols. Translated by Geoffrey W. Bromiley. Grand Rapids, MI: Eerdmans, 1997.

Feldman, Louis H. "The Omnipresence of the God-Fearers." *Biblical Archaeology Review* 12 no. 5 (Sept/Oct 1986): 58–69.

Feldman, Louis H. *Jew and Gentile in the Ancient World*. Princeton, NJ: Princeton University Press, 1993.

Fitzmyer, Joseph A. *The Acts of the Apostles: A New Translation with Introduction and Commentary*. New York, NY: Yale University Press, 1998.

Flusser, David and Huub van de Sandt . *The Didache: Its Jewish Sources and its Place in Early Judaism and Christianity*. Minneapolis, MN: Fortress Press, 2002.

Flusser, David and Shmuel Safrai. "Das Aposteldekret und die Noachitischen Gebote." Pages 176–192 in *Wer Tora vermehrt, mehrt Leben: Festgabe für Heinz Kremers*. Edited by E. Brocke and H.-J. Barkenings. Neukirchen-Vluyn, Germany: Neukirchener Verlag, 1986.

Flusser, David, *Judaism and the Origins of Christianity*. Jerusalem: Magnes Press, 1988.

Flusser, David. "Jewish-Christian Relations Past and Present." *Immanuel* 5 (Summer 1975): 74-48.

Flusser, David. *The Sage from Galilee: Rediscovering Jesus' Genius*. Grand Rapids, MI: Eerdmans, 2007.

Fonrobert, Charlotte Elisheva. *Menstrual Purity: Rabbinic and Christian Reconstructions of Biblical Gender*. Stanford, CA: Stanford University Press, 2002.

Goudoever, J. Van. *Biblical Calendars*. Leiden, Netherlands: Brill, 1961.

Hayes, Christine Elizabeth. *Gentile Impurities and Jewish Identities.* New York, NY: Oxford University Press, 2002.

Herczeg, Rabbi Yisrael Isser Zvi. *The Torah: With Rashi's Commentary Translated, Annotated, and Elucidated.* 5 vols. Brooklyn, NY: Mesorah Publications, 1994.

Hodge, C. *If Sons, Then Heirs: A Study of Kinship and Ethnicity in the Letters of Paul.* New York, NY: Oxford University Press, 2007.

Janicki, Toby. *Mezuzah: You Shall Write Them upon the Doorposts of Your House and Upon Your Gates.* Marshfield, MO: First Fruits of Zion, 2007.

Janicki, Toby. *Tefillin: A Study on the Commandment of Tefillin.* Marshfield, MO: First Fruits of Zion, 2010.

Janicki, Toby. *Tzitzit: You Shall Make for Yourselves Tassels on the Four Corners of the Garment.* Marshfield, MO: First Fruits of Zion, 2011.

Jastrow, Marcus. *Dictionary of Talmud Babli, Yerushalmi, Midrashic Literature and Targumim.* 2 vols. New York, NY: Pardes Publishing House, 1950.

Johnson, H. H. "The Acts, XV. 29." *The Classical Review* 33 nos. 5/6 (August/September 1919): 100–101.

Kellner, Menachem. *Maimonides on Judaism and the Jewish People.* Albany, NY: State University of New York Press, 1991.

Kittel, Gerhard, and Gerhard Friedrich, eds. *Theological Dictionary of the New Testament.* Translated by Geoffrey Bromiley. 10 vols. Grand Rapids, MI: Eerdmans, 1964–1974.

Lachs, Samuel T. *A Rabbinic Commentary on the New Testament.* New York, NY: KTAV Publishing House, 1987.

Lancaster, D. Thomas. "Something Off the Top of My Head." *Messiah Journal* 100 (Spring 2009): 50–66.

Lancaster, D. Thomas. *Grafted In.* Marshfield, MO: First Fruits of Zion, 2009.

Lancaster, D. Thomas. *The Holy Epistle to the Galatians: Sermons on a Messianic Jewish Approach.* Marshfield, MO: First Fruits of Zion, 2011.

Lancaster, D. Thomas. *Torah Club Volume Six: Chronicles of the Apostles.* Marshfield, MO: First Fruits of Zion, 2011.

Lancaster, D. Thomas. *Torah Club Volume Three: Voice of the Prophets*. Marshfield, MO: First Fruits of Zion, 2010.

Lauterbach, Jacob Z. *Mekhilta De-Rabbi Ishmael*. 2 vols. Philadelphia, PA: Jewish Publication Society, 2004.

LaSor, William Sanford. "Discovering What Jewish Miqva'ot Can Tell Us About Christian Baptism." *Biblical Archaeological Review* 13 no. 1 (1987): 52–59.

Levine, Baruch. *The JPS Torah Commentary: Leviticus*. Philadelphia, PA: Jewish Publication Society, 1991.

Levine, Elihu. *Kli Yakar*. 2 vols. Southfield, MI: Targum Press, 2007.

Lichtenstein, Dr. Aaron. *The Seven Laws of Noah*. Edison, NJ: Rabbi Jacob Joseph School Press, 1986.

Lieberman, Saul. *Greek in Jewish Palestine/Hellenism in Jewish Palestine*. New York, NY: Jewish Theological Seminary of America, 1994.

Lockshin, Martin. *Rashbam's Commentary on Leviticus and Numbers*. Providence, RI: Brown University, 2001.

Luria, Maxwell. *Elijah Benamozegh: Israel and Humanity*. Mahwah, NJ: Paulist Press, 1995.

Malinowitz, Rabbi Chaim, Rabbi Yisroel Simcha Schorr, and Rabbi Mordechai Marcus. *The Jerusalem Talmud: Tractate Peah*. Brooklyn, NY: Mesorah Publications, 2006.

Maloney, Robert P. "The Teaching of the Fathers on Usury: An Historical Study on the Development of Christian Thinking." *Vigiliae Christianae* 27 no. 4 (December 1973): 241–265.

Marcus, Ralph. "The *Sebomenoi* in Josephus." *Jewish Social Studies* 14 no. 3 (July 1952): 247–250.

Martindale, Wayne and Jerry Root. *The Quotable Lewis*. Carol Stream, IL: Tyndale Publishing House, 1990.

Michael, J. Hugh. "The Jewish Sabbath in the Latin Classical Writers." *The American Journal of Semitic Languages and Literatures* 40 no. 2 (January 1924): 117–124.

Milgrom, Jacob. *The JPS Torah Commentary: Numbers*. Philadelphia, PA: Jewish Publication Society, 1989.

Miller, Chris A. "Did Peter's Vision in Acts 10 Pertain to Men or the Menu?" *Bibliotheca Sacra* 159:635 (2002): 302–317.

Miller, Patrick M. *The Religion of Ancient Israel*. Louisville, KY: Westminster John Knox Press, 2000.

Moyes, Gordon. *"A Fresh Look at New Testament Baptism."* No Pages. Cited 30 November 2011. Online: http://www.gordonmoyes.com/wp-content/uploads//FreshLookatBaptism.pdf.

Murray, Michelle. *Playing a Jewish Game: Gentile Christian Judaizing in the First and Second Centuries CE*. Ontario, Canada: Wilfrid Laurier University Press, 2004.

Nanos, Mark. "Paul's *Reversal* of Jews Calling Gentiles 'Dogs' (Philippians 3:2): 1600 Years of an Ideological Tale Wagging an Exegetical Dog?" No pages. Cited 08 June 2009. Online: http://www.marknanos.com/Phil3Dogs-Reverse-1-17-08.pdf.

Nanos, Mark. *The Irony of Galatians: Paul's Letter in First-Century Context*. Minneapolis, MN: Fortress Press, 2002.

Nanos, Mark. *The Mystery of Romans*. Minneapolis, MN: Fortress Press, 1996.

Neusner, Jacob, ed. *The Jerusalem Talmud*. CD-ROM. Peabody, MA: Hendrickson Publishers, 2010.

Oswalt, John. *The New International Commentary on the Old Testament: The Book of Isaiah Chapters 40–66*. Grand Rapids, MI: Eerdmans, 1998.

Overman, Andrew J. "The God-fearers: Some Neglected Features." *Journal for the Study of the New Testament* 32 (1988): 17–26.

Paula Fredrickson, "Judaizing the Nations: The Ritual Demands of Paul's Gospel," *New Testament Studies* 56 (2010): 232–252.

Pines, Shlomo. "The Iranian Name for Christians and the 'God-Fearers.'" *Proceedings of the Israel Academy of Sciences and Humanities* 2 (1968): 143–152.

Polhill, John B. *The New American Commentary: Acts*. Nashville, TN: Broadman Press, 1992.

Rabinowitz, Rabbi Chaim Dov. *Da'ath Sofrim: Commentary to the Book of Yeshayahu*. New York, NY: H. Vagshal Publishing, 2006.

Rosner, Brian. *Paul, Scripture and Ethics: A Study of 1 Corinthians 5–7*. Leiden, The Netherlands: Brill, 1994.

Rudolph, David J. "The Celebration of Passover by Gentile Christians in the Patristic Period." *Verge* 2 no. 3 (2010): 4.

Sanders, Jack T. *Schismatics, Sectarians, Dissidents, Deviants: The First One Hundred Years of Jewish-Christian Relations.* Valley Forge, PA: Trinity Press International, 1993.

Sarna, Nahum. *The JPS Torah Commentary: Exodus.* Philadelphia, PA: The Jewish Publication Society, 1991.

Schonfeld, Rabbi Solomon. *The Universal Bible.* London: Sidgwick and Jackson, 1955.

Schwartz, Rabbi Yoel. "Noahide Commandments." Pages 235–292 in *Service from the Heart.* Edited by Rabbi Michael Katz, Rabbi Yechiel Sitzman, Pam Rogers, Larry Rogers, and Nancy January. Rose, OK: Oklahoma B'nai Noah Society, 2007.

Shulam, Joseph and Hilary Le Cornu. *A Commentary on the Jewish Roots of Acts.* 2 vols. Jerusalem: Academon, 2003.

Skarsaune, Oskar. *In the Shadow of the Temple.* Downers Grove, IL: InterVarsity Press, 2002.

Skolnik, Fred, Editor. *Encyclopaedia Judaica.* 2nd ed. 22 vols. Farmington Hills, MI: Macmillan Reference, 2006.

Tannenbaum, Robert. "Jews and God-Fearers in the Holy City of Aphrodite." *Biblical Archaeology Review* 12 no. 5 (Sept/Oct 1986): 54–57.

Tigay, Jeffery. *JPS Torah Commentary: Deuteronomy.* Philadelphia, PA: Jewish Publication Society, 1996.

Tomson, Peter. *Paul and Jewish Law.* Minneapolis, MN: Fortress Press, 1990.

Touger, Rabbi Eliyahu. *Maimonides Mishneh Torah.* 27 vols. Jerusalem: Moznaim Publishing, 1988.

Tucker, J. Brian. "God-Fearers: Literary Foil or Historical Reality in the Book of Acts." *Journal of Biblical Studies* 5 no. 1 (January 2005): 21–39.

Ulfgard, Hakan. *Feast and Future: Revelation 7:9–17 and the Feast of Tabernacles.* Lund, Sweden: Wallin and Dalholm, 1989.

Ulfgard, Hakan. *The Story of Sukkot: The Setting, Shaping, and Sequel of the Biblical Feast of Tabernacles.* Tubingen: Mohr Siebeck, 1998.

Weiss, Abraham. "Shevitat Akum." *Bar-Ilan Annual* 1 (1963): 143–148, xxxi–xxxii.

Zwecker, Tal Moshe. *Noam Elimelech*. Southfield, MI: Targum Press, 2008.

ENDNOTES

1   y.*Brachot* 9:2; b.*Menachot* 43b (Note: Some manuscripts have "who has made me an Israelite" instead.) Also t.*Brachot* 6:18. It is probable that it was recited in some form in the first century. Although the blessing "who has not made me a Gentile" seems to imply a low opinion of those from the nations, this blessing should not be understood as denigrating or condescending. As with the blessing "who has not made me a woman," the intent is to praise God for the obligation to perform the commandments—something traditional Judaism does not view as incumbent upon non-Jews and only partially incumbent on women.

2   Marcus Jastrow, "גוי," *Dictionary of Talmud Babli, Yerushalmi, Midrashic Literature and Targumim,* 1:220.

3   F. Brown, S. Driver, and C. Briggs, "גוי," *Brown-Driver-Briggs Hebrew and English Lexicon,* 156–157.

4   Cf. Esau in Genesis 21:18 and Jacob in Genesis 46:30.

5   Peter echoes this exact (Israel-specific) language for the Gentile believers in 1 Peter 2:9.

6   Clements, "גוי," *Theological Dictionary of the Old Testament,* 2:426–433.

7   Clements, 2:426–433.

8   b.*Avodah Zarah* 36b. See Theodore Friedman, "Gentile," *Encyclopedia Judaica* (2nd Edition) 7:485–487.

9   E.g., b.*Chagigah* 13a; *Exodus Rabbah* 47:1. The prohibition was generally seen as referring to the Oral Law.

10 Samuel T. Lachs, *A Rabbinic Commentary on the New Testament* (New York, NY: KTAV Publishing House, 1987), 138–140. E.g., *Song of Songs Rabbah* 1:7; b.*Chagigah* 3a.

11 *Genesis Rabbah* 55:1; *Leviticus Rabbah* 13:5. Philo of Alexandria calls some antagonists of Israel dogs (*Every Good Man Is Free,* 90). Note also that wicked of Israel are referred to as dogs as well in *Midrash Tehillim*

4 and the church father Ignatius refers to heretics as "ravenous dogs" (*Epistle of Ignatius to the Ephesians* 7:1). Therefore the term is not a racist one but rather a way to refer to the wicked and idolatrous. Cf. Philippians 3:2 and the discussion of Mark Nanos in "Paul's *Reversal* of Jews Calling Gentiles 'Dogs' (Philippians 3:2): 1600 Years of an Ideological Tale Wagging an Exegetical Dog?" n.p. [cited June 08, 2009]. Online: http://www.marknanos.com/Phil3Dogs-Reverse-1-17-08.pdf.

12 Lachs, *A Rabbinic Commentary on the New Testament*, 138–140.

13 Lachs, *A Rabbinic Commentary on the New Testament*, 249, cites a midrash that "compares the righteous to the guests at a wedding banquet invited to the king's table, and the wicked heathen to the dogs who obtain the crumbs that fall there from."

14 Wayne Martindale and Jerry Root, *The Quotable Lewis* (Carol Stream, IL: Tyndale Publishing House, 1990), 348.

15 There are a few other passages in Matthew where it appears that Yeshua speaks disparagingly of non-Jews as well; such as in 5:47, where he states that "if you greet only your brothers, what more are you doing than others? Do not even the Gentiles do the same?" "And when you pray, do not heap up empty phrases as the Gentiles do" (6:7). It should be noted though that in both those passages as well as in 18:17, the Greek word is *ethnikoi* (εθνικοι), whereas elsewhere when Matthew speaks of Gentiles he uses *ethnos* (εθνος) such as in 10:5. The word *ethnikoi* only appears in these three Matthean passages and in Galatians 2:14 and 3 John 7. Lachs writes, "It is likewise significant that Jerome, when translating the Matthean passages where *ethnikoi* appears, renders it by *ethnici*, while in Galatians 2:14 and 3 John 7, he translates it by *gentibus*. Presumably Jerome realized that *ethnikoi* was not employed by Matthew as a general term for the non-Jew; rather it designated a specific group within the Jewish people." He also points out that the Roman emperor Justinian uses *ethnikoi* to refer to the "provincials." Therefore he speculates that the term refers in Matthew to the rabbinic term *am ha'aretz* ("people of the land," עם הארץ), i.e., the Jewish population who were generally ignorant of the Torah. He further explains that "brothers" (αδελφους) in Matthew 5:47 would correspond to the Hebrew *chaver* ("associate, colleague," חבר) which is the antithesis to the *am ha'aretz* in the rabbinic world. See Lachs, *A Rabbinic Commentary on the New Testament*, 109–110 and Lachs, "Studies in the Semitic Background to the Gospel of Matthew," *Jewish Quarterly Review* 67 (1977): 195–217.

16 Luke 2:25–32.

17 William Sanford LaSor, "Discovering What Jewish Miqva'ot Can Tell Us About Christian Baptism," *Biblical Archeological Review* 13 no. 1 (1987): 52–59.

18   See Daniel Lancaster, *Grafted In* (Marshfield, MO: First Fruits of Zion, 2009).

19   *Didache* 9–10. See Jonathan Draper, "The Holy Vine of David Made Known to the Gentiles through God's Servant Jesus: 'Christian-Judaism' in the Didache," *Jewish Christianity Reconsidered* (Minneapolis, MN: Fortress Press, 2007), 257–283.

20   m.*Oholot* 18:7. Cf. Luke 7:6–7. The Gentile centurion probably assumed that the Master, as a Torah-observant Jewish sage, would not enter into a Gentile's house.

21   There is a church tradition Peter did not eat with Gentiles unless they repented and were immersed (*Clementine Homilies* 13:4).

22   *Ma'aseh* translates as "it once happened," see m.*Brachot* 1:1, 2:5; m.*Sukkah* 2:5; b.*Yevamot* 46b; Menachem Elon, *"Ma'aseh,"* *Encyclopedia Judaica* (2nd Edition), 13:308–312; and Joseph Shulam and Hilary Le Cornu, *A Commentary on the Jewish Roots of Acts* (Jerusalem: Academon, 2003), 609, 829–830.

23   The Master indicates this when he gives Peter "the keys of the kingdom of heaven" (Matthew 16:17–19) and then appears to him first after his resurrection (1 Corinthians 15:4).

24   Acts 15.

25   G. Abbott-Smith, "εθνος," *A Manual Greek Lexicon of the New Testament* 129–130.

26   Karl Ludwig Schmidt, *"εθνος, εθνικος,"* *Theological Dictionary of the Old Testament* 2:369-372.

27   See also 1 Corinthians 5:1, 12:2; 1 Peter 2:12; 1 John 3:7; and throughout Revelation.

28   See also Acts 15:23; Romans 16:4.

29   Yechiel Tzvi Lichtenstein, *Commentary on the Acts of the Apostles* (trans. Robert Morris; Marshfield, MO: Vine of David, forthcoming), on Acts 15:7.

30   Cf. *Mechilta, Nezikin* 18; b.*Chaggigah* 3a; y.*Bikkurim* 1:4; *Peskita Rabbati* 43:4.

31   Cf. 1 Clement 4. Also note Hodge who sees Romans 9:7 ("Not all are children of Abraham because they are his offspring, but, 'through Isaac shall your offspring be named'") as indicating that Gentiles are spiritually descended through Isaac (C. Hodge, *If Sons, Then Heirs: A Study of Kinship and Ethnicity in the Letters of Paul* [New York, NY: Oxford University Press, 2007], 94).

32   Mark Nanos, *The Mystery of Romans* (Minneapolis, MN: Fortress Press, 1996), 179–192.

33 David Flusser, *Judaism and the Origins of Christianity*, (Jerusalem: Magnes Press, 1988), 535–542.

34 Leviticus 21:17–24.

35 Numbers 4.

36 See "Appendix 1: Gentiles Observing Torah in Jewish Law" for more details on the Noachide Laws.

37 Exodus 12:38. Ibn Ezra also connects the "rabble" mentioned in Numbers 11:4 to the "mixed multitude" of the Exodus.

38 E.g., Exodus 23:12; Leviticus 19:10, 23:22, 25:6, 47–49.

39 There was the additional category of the *ger toshav* ("resident alien," גר), a Gentile who lived among ancient Israel and under legal protections from Israel which included receiving charity if necessary. According to the *Talmud*, they were required to make a formal proclamation renouncing idolatry before a Jewish court of law (*beit din*, בית דין) and then, according to one opinion, to keep all of the 613 commandments of the Torah with the exception of the prohibition to eat a *nevelah* (נבלה), i.e., an animal that has died of itself (b.*Avodah Zarah* 64b). The Talmud allows the *ger toshav* to eat *nevelah* because Deuteronomy 14:21 forbids an Israelite to eat the carcass of an animal that dies of itself, but it permits the Israelite to give it to a *ger* ("stranger," גר). There also appears to be a less formal type of *ger toshav* who does not make a formal declaration before a *beit din* and therefore is not legally eligible for protection and support (b.*Avodah Zarah* 65a).

40 See "Appendix 2: *Ger* as Proselyte."

41 Special thanks to Aaron Eby who helped significantly with the next three sections.

42 Nahum Sarna, *The JPS Torah Commentary: Exodus* (Philadelphia, PA: The Jewish Publication Society, 1991), 64.

43 Cf. Exodus 13:7.

44 Jacob Milgrom, *The JPS Torah Commentary: Numbers* (Philadelphia, PA: The Jewish Publication Society, 1989), 401.

45 This verse and the distinction it implied was quite troubling to the sages who interpreted *ger* as "proselyte." For a discussion of rabbinic interpretations of this passage, see Martin Lockshin, *Rashbam's Commentary on Leviticus and Numbers* (Providence, RI: Brown University, 2001), 124 n. 35.

46 Milgrom, 401.

47 Baruch Levine, *The JPS Torah Commentary: Leviticus* (Philadelphia, PA: The Jewish Publication Society, 1991), 168.

48 Exodus 23:12.

49   Ancient Judaism viewed the "foreigner" in this passage not as referring to a convert but rather to the *ger toshav* (b.*Yevamot* 48b). Cf. Genesis 9:3.

50   Milgrom, 401.

51   Patrick M. Miller, *The Religion of Ancient Israel* (Louisville, KY: Westminster John Knox Press, 2000), 201.

52   Tomson, 271–272.

53   "Judaism recognizes equality of rights for the non-Jewish God-fearers as far as salvation is concerned. There were of course social barriers: for God-fearers could not marry Jews" (David Flusser, "Jewish-Christian Relations Past and Present," *Immanuel* 5 [Summer 1975]: 74-48).

54   Louis H. Feldman, *Jew and Gentile in the Ancient World* (Princeton, NJ: Princeton University Press, 1993), 342. It could also be used to refer to Jews at times.

55   J. Brian Tucker, "God-Fearers: Literary Foil or Historical Reality in the Book of Acts," *Journal of Biblical Studies* 5 no. 1 (January 2005): 21–39. According to Acts 13:43 it could even at times refer to full proselytes.

56   Shlomo Pines, "The Iranian Name for Christians and the 'God-Fearers,'" *Proceedings of the Israel Academy of Sciences and Humanities* 2 (1968): 143–152.

57   Cf. Malachi 3:17 and the LXX version of 1 Chronicles 5:6: "those gathered about them." See Andrew J. Overman, "The God-fearers: Some Neglected Features," *Journal for the Study of the New Testament* 32 (1988): 17–26. Also note that Job is described to as "one who feared God" (Job 1:1). While the sages debated whether or not Job was Jewish or Gentile (e.g., b.*Bava Batra* 15a), most scholars are of the opinion that he was an Edomite.

58   For a full survey of the literary and archaeological evidence for the God-fearers see Feldman, *Jew and Gentile in the Ancient World*, 342–382, and Louis H. Feldman, "The Omnipresence of the God-Fearers," *Biblical Archaeology Review* 12 no. 5 (Sept/Oct 1986): 58–69.

59   For a full treatment of God-fearers in rabbinic literature see Saul Lieberman, *Greek in Jewish Palestine/ Hellenism in Jewish Palestine* (New York, NY: Jewish Theological Seminary of America, 1994), 77–90, and Bernard J. Bamberger, *Proselytism in the Talmudic Period* (New York, NY: KTAV Publishing House, 1968), 133–140.

60   b.*Sanhedrin* 70b; *Deuteronomy Rabbah* 2:24. Cf. y.*Megillah* 2:3. Josephus puts Nero's ill-fated wife Poppea in the category (*Antiquities* 20:195).

61   Josephus, *Wars of the Jews* 7:45. See also Ralph Marcus, "The *Sebomenoi* in Josephus," *Jewish Social Studies* 14 no. 3 (July 1952): 247–250.

62   Arrian, *Dissertationes* 2:19–21. See Feldman, "The Omnipresence of the God-Fearers," 60.

63   The opinion that Juvenal refers to God-fearers is found in Feldman, *Jew and Gentile in the Ancient World*, 347–348, and Feldman, "The Omnipresence of the God-Fearers," 61. Since Juvenal wrote late in the first century, there is reason to believe that the God-fearers he spoke of might have been believers in Yeshua.

64   Robert Tannenbaum, "Jews and God-Fearers in the Holy City of Aphrodite," *Biblical Archaeology Review* 12 no. 5 (Sept/Oct 1986): 54–57.

65   Pines, 148.

66   For example Chris A. Miller suggests Peter would have been keeping kosher on some level as well. See "Did Peter's Vision in Acts 10 Pertain to Men or the Menu?" *Bibliotheca Sacra* 159:635 (2002): 302–317.

67   Acts 13:50, 16:14, 17:17, 18:7.

68   Pines, 146–147.

69   Pines, 151.

70   David Flusser, "Jewish-Christian Relations Past and Present," 48-74.

71   David Flusser, *Judaism and the Origins of Christianity*, 630.

72   Romans 2:29.

73   Cf. Deuteronomy 5:27.

74   "The four prohibitions of the apostolic decree have generated a remarkable amount of manuscript variants. The four prohibitions appear in different orders in different manuscripts. In some cases, early scribes and copyists attempted to clarify the obscurity of the passage and, by doing so, wrote their own interpretations into the manuscripts. In other cases, copyists found the list unsatisfactory and sought to augment it, or in some cases, diminish it. Scribes of the Western tradition did not like the dietary laws and chose to omit the prohibition on 'what is strangled.' One manuscript omits the prohibition on sexual immorality, and some add a form of the Golden Rule: 'And whatever they do not wish to be done to them, they should not do to others.' Readers can sympathize with the scribe who originally tried to improve the text by adding the Golden Rule. The four laws seem to leave out a lot of important and obviously obligatory commandments such as honoring one's parents, basic integrity, prohibitions on theft, and so forth. Puzzlement over the four laws persists in the academic community today where textual critics propose various emendations and 'corrections.' For

example, many wonder why three out of the four requirements are dietary in nature. Most scholars agree that the original form of the apostolic decree had all four prohibitions and no Golden Rule. It is easy to see why Christian scribes objected to the ceremonial laws and attempted to improve the list, but a Christian scribe would be unlikely to introduce Old Testament dietary prohibitions into the text" (D. Thomas Lancaster, *Torah Club Volume Six: Chronicles of the Apostles* (Marshfield, MO: First Fruits of Zion, 2011) on *Parashat Mishpatim*). David Flusser and Shmuel Safrai redact the text to reflect Judaism's three, non-negotiable prohibitions: idolatry, adultery, and murder. Their argument requires understanding the specific charge against "things polluted by idols" as idolatry in general and the word "blood" as "bloodshed." It also requires completely omitting "things strangled." The entire argument is based anachronistically on a decision made in Lydda several decades after the Jerusalem council: "By a majority vote, it was resolved in the upper chambers of the house of Nithza in Lydda that in every other law of the Torah, if a man is commanded, 'Either break this commandment or you will die,' he may break any commandment to save his life except idolatry, incest, and murder" (b.*Sanhedrin* 74a). See David Flusser and Shmuel Safrai, "Das Aposteldekret und die Noachitischen Gebote," in E. Brocke and H.-J. Barkenings, eds., *Wer Tora vermehrt, mehrt Leben: Festgabe für Heinz Kremers* (Neukirchen-Vluyn: Neukirchener Verlag, 1986), 176–192). There is an interesting parallel to these four injunctions found in the *Quran*: "Prohibited to you are dead animals, blood, the flesh of swine, and that which has been dedicated to other than Allah, and [those animals] killed by strangling or by a violent blow or by a headlong fall or by the goring of horns, and those from which a wild animal has eaten, except what you [are able to] slaughter [before its death], and those which are sacrificed on stone altars, and [prohibited is] that you seek decision through divining arrows" (5:3).

75   Exodus 34:15.

76   See also Revelation 2:14, 20.

77   Tomson, 180–181.

78   E.g., 1 Corinthians 12:2 and 1 Thessalonians 1:9–10.

79   Paul Barnett, *The New International Commentary on the New Testament: The Second Epistle to the Corinthians* (Grand Rapids, MI: Eerdmans, 1997), 350.

80   Paula Fredrickson, "Judaizing the Nations: The Ritual Demands of Paul's Gospel," *New Testament Studies* 56 (2010): 232–252.

81   Origen, *Against Celsus* 4:31; see David W. Bercot, *A Dictionary of Early Christian Beliefs* (Peabody, MA: Hendrickson Publishers, 1998), 351–354.

82   Reiner Sörries, "Images," *The Encyclopedia of Christianity* 658–660.

83   There is a parallel practice in the early church that is now only practiced in Greek Orthodox circles of woman refraining from taking communion during their menstrual cycle. See Charlotte Elisheva Fonrobert, *Menstrual Purity: Rabbinic and Christian Reconstructions of Biblical Gender* (Stanford, CA: Stanford University Press, 2002).

84   Judaism interpreted this as including married woman covering their heads and there is evidence that such was the practice of the early church (e.g., 1 Corinthians 11:1–6; Tertullian, *On Veiling Virgins*). See D. Thomas Lancaster, "Something Off the Top of My Head," *Messiah Journal* 100 (Spring 2009): 50–66.

85   Cf. 1 Timothy 2:9–10 and 1 Corinthians 7:1–2.

86   E.g., 1 Corinthians 7:10ff.; Romans 7:2ff.

87   E.g., Genesis 34:31, 38:24; Leviticus 19:29, 21:7, 9, 14; Numbers 25:1; Deuteronomy 22:21.

88   John B. Polhill, *The New American Commentary: Acts* (Nashville, TN: Broadman Press, 1992), 330.

89   Joseph A. Fitzmyer, *The Acts of the Apostles: A New Translation with Introduction and Commentary* (New York, NY: Yale University Press, 1998), 557.

90   Tomson, 178–179.

91   "'Things strangled' (πνικτων) are prohibited in Leviticus 17:13. The difficulty with this term in the apostolic decree has arisen simply because Leviticus 17:13 is a positive prescription: that animals killed for eating must be slaughtered in such a way that their blood drains out. Abstention from πνικτων is the negative corollary, for an animal killed in such a way that the blood remains 'choked.'" See Richard Bauckham, *The Book of Acts in its First Century Setting, Volume 4: Palestinian Setting* (Grand Rapids, MI: Eerdmans, 1995), 459.

92   m.*Chullin* 1:2. In Acts 10:14, Peter may be referring to the fact that he has never eaten meat that has not been ritually slaughtered when he states "I have never eaten anything that is common [*chullin*, חולין]." Joseph Shulam writes: "Since *chullin* may also refer to the manner in which unconsecrated animals are slaughtered, Peter may be implying that he has never eaten anything which has been improperly slaughtered according to the halakhot of *chullin*." See Shulam and Le Cornu, *A Commentary on the Jewish Roots of Acts*, 1:566.

93   Philo, *The Special Law* 4:122; *Joseph and Aseneth* 8:5.

94   Polhill, *The New American Commentary: Acts*, 330.

95   Jeffery Tigay, *JPS Torah Commentary: Deuteronomy* (Philadelphia, PA: Jewish Publication Society, 1996), 125.

96   Oskar Skarsaune, *In the Shadow of the Temple* (Downers Grove, IL: InterVarsity Press, 2002), 239.

97   Many scholars have been puzzled as to why there are three dietary laws and one that is not and therefore have proposed theories as to what *porneia* actually was originally in this context. At least one scholar has suggested emending *porneia* ("sexual immorality," πορνεια) to *porkeia* ("food made of pork," πορκεια), thereby making all of the prohibitions dietary in nature. See H. H. Johnson, "The Acts, XV. 29," *The Classical Review* 33 nos. 5/6 (August/ September 1919): 100–101.

98   Miller, "Did Peter's Vision in Acts 10 Pertain to Men or the Menu?" 302–317.

99   Michelle Murray, *Playing a Jewish Game: Gentile Christian Judaizing in the First and Second Centuries CE* (Ontario, Canada: Wilfrid Laurier University Press, 2004), 62. Murray also writes of a separate Eucharist service that took place in Philadelphia among the early believers. "The Situation in Philadelphia, according to Ignatius, was one in which people whom I identity as Gentile Christians were teaching Judaism (Phld. 6.1) and were relying too heavily on the Hebrew scripture (Phld. 8.2). It seems furthermore that they held a separate Eucharist service (Phld. 4.1) from the one in which Ignatius was involved." She then adds in a footnote: "Sanders suggests that the existence of a separate Eucharist was over concern of Jewish Dietary laws (Jack T. Sanders, *Schismatics, Sectarians, Dissidents, Deviants: The First One Hundred Years of Jewish-Christian Relations* (Valley Forge, PA: Trinity Press International, 1993, 188)." (90).

100 For more on Gentiles and kosher see Aaron Eby, *Biblically Kosher: A Messianic Jewish Perspective on Kashrut* (Marshfield, MO: First Fruits of Zion, 2012), 142–155.

101 D. Thomas Lancaster, *The Holy Epistle to the Galatians: Sermons on a Messianic Jewish Approach* (Marshfield, MO: First Fruits of Zion, 2011), 252–253.

102 Cf. Colossians 3:20.

103 b.*Kiddushin* 31a.

104 b.*Kiddushin* 32b.

105 1 Timothy 6:20; 1 Peter 2:1.

106 Jude 1:8–10; 1 Timothy 1:20.

107 1 Corinthians 16:1–4; 2 Corinthians 8:7–15, 9:7.

108 2 Timothy 2:15, 3:16–17, 4:1–4; Romans 15:4; Colossians 3:16; 1 Timothy 3:15, 4:15; Colossians 3:16.

109 Ephesians 5:28–32; 1 Corinthians 6:15–17.

110 Romans 12:13, 20; 3 John 1:5-8; 1 Peter 4:9.

111 Cf. 1 Corinthians 9:7–10.

112 Luke 10:29–37.

113 Tertullian, *Against Marcion* 17; *Apostolic Constitutions* 47:44. For a full treatment of the topic see Robert P. Maloney, "The Teaching of the Fathers on Usury: An Historical Study on the Development of Christian Thinking," *Vigiliae Christianae* 27 no. 4 (December 1973): 241–265.

114 See m.*Middot* 2:3; Josephus, *Jewish War* 5:5:2; and Josephus, *Antiquities* 15:11:5. Paula Fredrickson actually argues that the court of the Gentiles is what gave Paul his imagery for what Gentile participation in Israel looks like (Fredrickson, 232–252).

115 Cf. b.*Nazir* 62a.

116 m.*Shekalim* 1:5.

117 b.*T'rumah* 7a.

118 See also 1 Corinthians 15:20–23, 16:15; 1 Clement 29:1–3, 30:1.

119 *Didache* 13.

120 See Christine Elizabeth Hayes, *Gentile Impurities and Jewish Identities* (New York, NY: Oxford University Press, 2002), 109ff.

121 *Clementine Homilies* 13:4.

122 Numbers 19:11–22.

123 Gordon Moyes, "*A Fresh Look at New Testament Baptism*," n.p. [cited 30 November 2011]. Online: http://www.gordonmoyes.com/wp-content/uploads//FreshLookatBaptism.pdf .

124 *Canons of Hippolytus* 21.

125 E.g., *Canons of Hippolytus* 41. Also note "I desire then that in every place the men should pray, lifting holy hands" (1 Timothy 2:8). Paul's language of "lifting holy hands" echoes rabbinic language for the practice of the ritual washing of hands, *netilat yadayim* (נטילת ידים), literally "lifting hands." This may not just be a metaphorical reference to *netilat yadayim* but an allusion to the literal practice in the early Gentile communities.

126 Bernard Drachman and Kaufmann Kohler, "Ablution," *Jewish Encyclopedia* 1:68–71. See also Eusebius, *Church History* 10:4:40.

127 Charles B. Chavel, *Maimonides the Commandments Volume One: Positive* (New York, NY: Soncino Press, 1967), 8–9.

128 b.*Ta'anit* 2a.

129 *Didache* 8:3. Later Christian writers would interpret this as the "third," "sixth," and "ninth" hours (Tertullian, *On Prayer* 25; Clement of Alexandria, *Stromata* 7:7). These were based on Acts 2:15, 3:1, 10:3–9,

30, 16:25, 27:35. Still another tradition developed of praying seven times a day based on Psalm 119:164: "Seven times a day I praise you." This later practice can still be found in some liturgical churches today.

130 *Apostolic Constitutions* 7:34–38.

131 Christian liturgical tradition keeps "Canonical Hours" at first hour (sunrise; 6:00 AM), third hour (9:00 AM), sixth hour (12:00 PM), ninth hour (3:00 PM), twelfth hour (sunset; 6:00 PM), compline (bedtime), and in some monastic traditions, midnight. Each of these corresponds to a major or minor time of prayer in Jewish practice.

132 The sages also drew a conclusion to bless before the meal based upon blessing after the meal through the argument of *kal va-chomer* [inference from a minor to a major], "If he says a blessing when he is full, how much more so ought he to do so when he is hungry?" (b.*Brachot* 35a)

133 1 Corinthians 10:25–26.

134 See b.*Pesachim* 107a; b.*Sotah* 38b.

135 *Didache* 9–10.

136 See Huub van der Sandt and David Flusser, *The Didache: Its Jewish Sources and its Place in Early Judaism and Christianity* (Minneapolis, MN: Fortress Press, 2002), 310–325. Draper sees the "poetic expansion" of these prayers as similar to what later became known as *piyyutim* in Jewish circles. See Draper's chapter in *Jewish Christianity Reconsidered*, 272.

137 Exodus 31:13, 17.

138 Exodus 13:9; Deuteronomy 6:8, 11:18.

139 Genesis 17:11.

140 Deuteronomy 6:9, 11:19.

141 Numbers 15:39.

142 Some might be inclined to also include *peyot* (side locks) and beards in this category as well. Both of these practices are based on interpretations of Leviticus 19:27: "You shall not round off the hair on your temples or mar the edges of your beard." It is significant that the early church fathers spoke harshly against those who shaved or marred their beards and accused them of violating the Leviticus commandment. See Bercot, 66–67.

143 Rambam, *Mishneh Torah, Milah* 3:7. See also *Responsa of the Rambam*, siman 148.

144 For further reading see Rabbi Solomon Schonfeld, *The Universal Bible* (London: Sidgwick and Jackson, 1955).

145 Some scholars suggest that the seventh-day Sabbath is related to the Babylonian mid-month celebration of the new moon called *šapattu*

and the Babylonian seven-day intervals, yet this remains speculative and unfounded.

146 Sarna, 15.

147 Rabbi Chayim ben Attar, *Or HaChayim: Commentary on the Torah* (5 vols.; trans. Eliyahu Munk; New York, NY: Lambda Publishers, 1999), 1:47.

148 *Midrash Rabbah* relates a tradition that the Israelites kept Shabbat in Egypt (*Exodus Rabbah* 1:28, 5:18). Exodus 16:23 may even allude to the Israelites observing Shabbat according to an unwritten oral tradition. The text literally states: "And [Moses] said unto them, 'It is that which the LORD has spoken of; a rest, a holy Sabbath to the LORD is tomorrow.'" The phrase "It is that" is the Hebrew word *hu* (הוא), perhaps referring to something in the past. Perhaps Moses refers to "that" which the Israelites already knew.

149 Rabbi Attar, 51.

150 *Genesis Rabbah* 22:13.

151 Translation from Rabbi Yisrael Isser Zvi Herczeg, *The Torah: With Rashi's Commentary Translated, Annotated, and Elucidated* (5 vols.; Brooklyn, NY: Mesorah Publications, 1994), 2:442.

152 Elchanan Adler, "The Sabbath Observing Gentile: Halakhic, Hashkafic and Liturgical Responses," *Tradition* 36 no. 3 (2002): 14–45.

153 b.*Yevamot* 48b.

154 See "Appendix 1: Gentiles Observing Torah in Jewish Law" for more details on the *ger toshav*.

155 See Rashi's commentary to b.*Yevamot* 48a.

156 *Mishneh Torah*, *Issurei Bi'ah* 14:8.

157 Rabbi Yoel Schwartz, "Noahide Commandments," in *Service from the Heart* (ed. Rabbi Michael Katz et al.; Rose, OK: Oklahoma B'nai Noah Society, 2007), 235–292.

158 My exegesis of Isaiah 56 relies heavily on *Torah Club Volume Three, Voice of the Prophets* (Marshfield, MO: First Fruits of Zion, 2010), commenting on *Ta'anit Tzibbur Minchah*.

159 Rabbi Chaim Dov Rabinowitz, *Da'ath Sofrim: Commentary to the Book of Yeshayahu* (New York, NY: H. Vagshal Publishing, 2006), 471.

160 See "Appendix 2: *Ger* as Proselyte."

161 John Oswalt, *The New International Commentary on the Old Testament: The Book of Isaiah Chapters 40–66* (Grand Rapids, MI: Eerdmans, 1998), 458.

162 Samuele Bacchiocchi, *From Sabbath to Sunday: A Historical Investigation of the Rise of Sunday Observance in Early Christianity* (Rome: The Pontifical Gregorian University Press, 1977), 74–131.

163 Cf. David Flusser, *Judaism and the Origins of Christianity*, 630.

164 E.g., Acts 13:16, 44, 14:1.

165 Schaller, 4:788–791.

166 Josephus, *Against Apion* 2:40; J. Hugh Michael, "The Jewish Sabbath in the Latin Classical Writers," *The American Journal of Semitic Languages and Literatures* 40 no. 2 (January 1924): 117–124.

167 For an alternate but pro-Torah interpretation of Colossians 2 see Eby, 47–56.

168 Schaller, 4:788–791.

169 Angelos Chaniotis, "Godfearers in the City of Love," *Biblical Archaeology Review* 36 no. 3 (May/June 2010): 32–44, 77.

170 For a detailed and thorough study of this progression see Bacchiocchi, *From Sabbath to Sunday*.

171 The day in the biblical calendar starts in the evening and not at midnight as in Roman reckoning, therefore darkness on Saturday announced the beginning of the first day of the week. E.g., Acts 20:7; 1 Corinthians 16:2.

172 Bacchiocchi, 213–235.

173 *The Epistle of Ignatius to the Magnesians* 9.

174 See Emil G. Hirsch and Judah David Eisenstein, "Gentile," *Jewish Encyclopedia* 5:615–626. Note that the common phrase for "[neglecting] the words of the Rabbis one deserves death" (b.*Eruvin* 21b). See also *Mishneh Torah, Melachim* 10:9 and Chaim Clorfene and Yaakov Rogalsky, *The Path of the Righteous Gentile* (Southfield, MI: Targum Press, 1987), 42.

175 Friedman, "Gentile," 7:486. Also Hirsch and Eisenstein, "Gentile," 5:615–626 and Weiss, 143–148, xxxi–xxxii. Maimonides makes a similar proscription about a Gentile observing Shabbat deserving death (*Mishneh Torah, Melachim* 10:9). Once again though, it appears that Maimonides is speaking of the idolater and not the God-fearing Gentile. The Chatam Sofer (1762–1839) observes, "See Rambam, Laws of Kings, chapter 10, halachah 9 and 10, where it appears that he distinguishes between an idol worshipper and a Ben Noach, who is one that has accepted upon himself not to be an idolater; and for such a person it is permitted to cease [from work on the Sabbath] and to fulfill any commandment that he desires; and from such a person they accept sacrificial offerings, teach him Torah, and accept charity from him" (Commentary on b.*Chullin* 18a).

176 Weiss, xxxi.

177 Schwartz, 262.

178 Schwartz, 262.

179 Rabbi Meir Dan Polachi, *Chemdat Yisrael*, 227.

180 Shmuley Boteach, *Judaism for Everyone: Renewing Your Life through Vibrant Lessons of the Jewish Faith* (New York, NY: Basic Books, 2002), 3.

181 Daniel Stökl Ben Ezra, "Christians Observing 'Jewish' Festivals of Autumn," in *The Image of Judaeo- Christians in Ancient Jewish and Christian Literature* (eds. Peter J. Tomson and Doris Lambers-Petry; Tubingen, Germany: Moher Siebeck, 2003), 53–73.

182 Ben Ezra, 60.

183 For an alternate but pro-Torah perspective on both the Colossians 2 and Romans 14 passages see Eby, 47–65.

184 1 Corinthians 10:14.

185 Ben Ezra also states, "It is difficult to explain the observance of 'special years' in the Diaspora since the Jubilee and the Sabbatical year are valid only for the Land of Israel" ("Christians Observing 'Jewish' Festivals of Autumn," 59).

186 Mark Nanos, *The Irony of Galatians: Paul's Letter in First-century Context* (Minneapolis, MN: Fortress Press, 2002), 268.

187 Nanos, 268.

188 Furthermore, Rambam in his *Mishneh Torah* writes, "[Gentiles] are not allowed to originate a new religion or create mitzvot for themselves based on their own decisions" (*Melachim* 10:9 [Touger]). Although we cannot be sure, it would seem that a similar sentiment would have been present in the Second-Temple period and that the apostles would have frowned on the Gentiles creating new festivals.

189 Ephesians 2:12–13.

190 Brian Rosner, *Paul, Scripture and Ethics: A Study of 1 Corinthians 5–7* (Leiden, The Netherlands: Brill, 1994), 79–80.

191 David J. Rudolph, "The Celebration of Passover by Gentile Christians in the Patristic Period," *Verge* 2 no. 3 (2010): 4.

192 "Quartodecimanism," *The Oxford Dictionary of the Christian Church* 1364–1365. See also J. Van Goudoever, *Biblical Calendars* (Leiden, Netherlands: Brill, 1961), 155–163.

193 Goudoever, 176–181.

194 Goudoever, 178.

195 *Mekhilta De-Rabbi Shimon bar Yochai* on Exodus 12:45. Cf. b.*Pesachim* 92a.

196 Exodus 34:23 and Deuteronomy 16:16.

197 Compare Colossians 4:10–11, 14.

198 Ben Ezra, "Christians Observing 'Jewish' Festivals of Autumn," 63.

199 Acts 21:27–29. Cf. Acts 20:4.

200 Goudoever, 182.

201 *Fragments of Irenaeus* 7.

202 *On Baptism* 19.

203 Ben Ezra, "Christians Observing 'Jewish' Festivals of Autumn," 62.

204 *Epistle to Diognetus* 4.

205 Ben Ezra, "Christians Observing 'Jewish' Festivals of Autumn," 69.

206 *Against the Jews* 1:5.

207 Daniel Stökl Ben Ezra, "Whose Fast is It? The Ember Day of September and Yom Kippur," in *The Ways That Never Parted* (eds. Adam H. Becker and Annette Yoshiko Reed; Tubingen, Germany: Moher Siebeck, 2003), 259–282.

208 Zechariah 14:16–19.

209 Leviticus 23:40. See m.*Sukkah* 3:1ff.

210 *Midrash Tehillim* 21; Rashi to *Zechariah* 14:16–19. Cf. y.*Avodah Zarah* 2:1.

211 m.*Sukkah* 4:9.

212 Hakan Ulfgard, *Feast and Future: Revelation 7:9–17 and the Feast of Tabernacles* (Lund: Wallin and Dalholm, 1989). Also see Hakan Ulfgard, *The Story of Sukkot: The Setting, Shaping, and Sequel of the Biblical Feast of Tabernacles* (Tubingen: Mohr Siebeck, 1998), 274–279 for a detailed discussion of later church fathers' eschatological interpretations of Sukkot.

213 Goudoever, 214; see also 210–213.

214 *Against the Jews* 9:2.

215 Jean Danielou, *The Theology of Jewish Christianity* (John A. Baker, trans.; Philadelphia, PA: Darton, Longman and Todd, 1978), 343.

216 In fact, Louis Feldmen points out that one of the major attractions of non-Jews to Judaism was the celebration of Jewish festivals. See Louis Feldmen, *Jew and Gentile in the Ancient World*, 376–377.

217 t.*Avodah Zarah* 2:4; Yehudah B. Cohn, *Tangled Up in Text: Tefillin and the Ancient World* (Providence, RI: Brown Judaic Studies, 2008), 124

218 *Mechilta, Pischa* 17; y. *Eruvin* 10:3.

219 For example see *Mishneh Torah, Hilchot Tzitzit* 3:9.

220 y.*Avodah Zarah* 2:1; *Midrash Tehillim* 21.

221 b.*Menachot* 43a.

222 *Mishneh Torah, Hilchot Tzitzit* 3:9.

223 Some such as Rabbi Yoel Schwartz say it is permissible but that they must be tied in such as way that does not confuse them with Jewish ones. See *Schwartz*, 303.

224 y.*Peah* 1:1, 7b.

225 b.*Bava Metzia* 102a.

226 Lancaster, *The Holy Epistle to the Galatians*, 194.

227 b.*Bava Kamma* 113b. Also see proselytes (προσηλυτος) mentioned in Matthew 23:15 and Acts 2:11, 6:5, 13:43.

228 See b.*Avodah Zarah* 64b. The reasoning behind the *ger toshav* being permitted to eat a *nevelah* is because, in Deuteronomy 14:21, while an Israelite is forbidden to eat a carcass of an animal that dies of itself, he is permitted to give it to a *ger* ("stranger," גר). There also appears to be a less formal type of *ger toshav* who does not make a formal declaration before a *beit din* and therefore he is not legally eligible for protection and support (b.*Avodah Zarah* 65a).

229 *Mishneh Torah, Issurei Bi'ah* 14:7.

230 *Mishneh Torah, Issurei Bi'ah* 14:8.

231 E.g., b.*Sanhedrin* 56aff.; t.*Avodah Zarah* 8:4ff. For a contemporary discussion of these laws see Clorfene and Rogalsky, 40–47.

232 Cf. *Jubilees* 7 for an earlier formulation: "That they might do justice and cover the shame of their flesh and bless the one who created them and honor father and mother, and each one love his neighbor and preserve themselves from fornication and pollution and from all injustice … covering [the blood] which will be poured out upon the surface of the earth. And you shall not be like the one who eats with blood, but beware lest they should eat blood before you. Cover the blood … And you shall not eat living flesh."

233 See b.*Sanhedrin* 57a; b.*Chullin* 92a; t.*Avodah Zarah* 8:6; Rambam, *Mishneh Torah, Hilchot Melachim* 10:6. See also Clorfene and Rogalsky, 44–47.

234 *Genesis Rabbah* 98:9; y.*Avodah Zarah* 2:1; *Midrash Tehillim* 21. Dr. Aaron Lichtenstein makes the case that the seven Noachide laws actually divide up into sixty subdivisions (fifty-two positive and fourteen negative) in his book *The Seven Laws of Noah* (Edison, NJ: Rabbi Jacob Joseph School Press, 1986). See also *Mishneh Torah, Hilchot Melachim* 9:9 for a breakdown of the prohibition of robbery.

235 A notable exception to this opinion was Rabbi Elijah ben Abraham Benamozegh who believed that while Gentiles observed the seven laws of Noah, they should follow their own religious customs and practices, e.g., a modified version of Catholicism, etc. See Maxwell Luria, *Elijah Benamozegh: Israel and Humanity* (Mahwah, NJ: Paulist Press, 1995). This seems to contrast with Rambam who writes that

Gentiles are not to "originate a new religion or create mitzvot for themselves based on their own decisions" (*Mishneh Torah, Melachim* 10:9 [Touger]).

236 b.*Kiddushin* 31a; b.*Avodah Zarah* 23b–24a; y.*Peah* 1:1, 5b–6a.

237 Also *Deuteronomy Rabbah* 1:21.

238 See Hirsch and Eisenstein, "Gentile," 5:615–626. Note the common phrase: "for [neglecting] the words of the Rabbis one deserves death" (b.*Eruvin* 21b [Soncino]). See also *Mishneh Torah, Melachim* 10:9 and Clorfene and Roglasky, 42.

239 b.*Avodah Zarah* 3a and b.*Bava Kamma* 38a.

240 Friedman, "Gentile," 7:486. Also Hirsch and Eisenstein, "Gentile," 5:615–626 and Weiss, 143–148, xxxi–xxxii.

241 b.*Gittin* 45b; b.*Menachot* 42b.

242 y.*Peah* 1:1, 7b.

243 Perhaps in response to the discomfort of a Gentile being given a mezuzah, commentator *Pnei Moshe* states that Artaban was actually a prominent Jew. See Rabbi Chaim Malinowtiz, Rabbi Yisroel Simcha Schorr, and Rabbi Mordechai Marcus, *The Jerusalem Talmud: Tractate Peah* (Brooklyn, NY: Mesorah Publications, 2006), 7b2 n. 19. According to the Rabbi Moses Isserles in his comments to the *Shulhan Aruch*, *Yoreh Deah* 292:2, it is permissible to send a Gentile a mezuzah if there is fear that if one does not it may cause hatred. Yet in the Talmudic case there is a friendly relationship between Rabbi Yehudah and Artaban, so this would not apply.

244 b.*Bava Metzia* 102a.

245 *Mishneh Torah, Tzitzit* 3:9. Additionally authentic *techelet* should not be left with a Gentile (*Mishneh Torah, Tzitzit* 2:6) and "if he purchases [a garment with tzitzit] from a gentile merchant, it is [presumed to be] acceptable; from a non-Jew who is a private person, it is not acceptable" (*Mishneh Torah, Tzitzit* 2:7 [Touger]).

246 *Mishneh Torah, Tefillin* 1:11, 13; 3:16.

247 Note that Rabbi David ben Shlomo ibn Avi Zimra ("the Radbaz," a famous commentator on Rambam's text) comments on this passage and states that "mitzvot which require holiness and purity, for example, tefillin or mezuzah, should be withheld from gentiles" (Rabbi Eliyahu Touger, *Maimonides Mishneh Torah: Sefer Shoftim* [Jerusalem: Moznaim Publishing, 1988], 604 n. 65). It should be noted, however, that this is commentary on Rambam's work and that the Rambam himself makes no mention of these exceptions. Additionally some have noted that the original Hebrew of the Radbaz's statement (*chochech*, חוכך) might be better expressed as stating hesitation rather than outright prohibition and that the issue surrounds Gentiles

making tefillin and mezuzah rather than practicing them. This would be in accordance with Rambam—elsewhere he forbids a non-Jew from making tefillin (*Mishneh Torah, Tefillin* 1:11, 13; 3:16). So while Rambam does say that Gentiles cannot make tefillin, he never states that they cannot wear them, although presumably he would state that they should be worn without the blessing "who has commanded us," for he would feel that a Gentile is not commanded to wrap tefillin (cf. *Mishneh Torah, Tzitzit* 3:9).

248 Yet according to the Talmudic dictum, "Greater is the reward of those who having been enjoined do good deeds than of those who not having been enjoined [but merely out of free will] do good deeds," the reward for observance of non-obligatory commandments would be less than if one was obligated (b.*Kiddushin* 31a and b.*Avodah Zarah* 3a). Nevertheless, Abraham, Isaac, and Jacob are considered to be on this level. "Even though unto them the Torah had not yet been given, they fulfilled it of their own accord" (*Leviticus Rabbah* 2:10). See also Rabbi Elimelech, *Noam Elimelech* (Southfield, MI: Targum Press, 2008), 211. For the suggestion that Rambam is only permitting casual and irregular observance of the commandments for Gentiles see Adler, "The Sabbath Observing Gentile: Halakhic, Hashkafic and Liturgical Responses," 39 n. 29.

249 Commentary on b.*Chullin* 18a. The *Avnei Shoham* seeks to resolve the seeming contradiction by stating that in section 9 the Rambam is referring to commandments Gentiles make up or invent whereas in section 10 he refers to the observance of the 613 commandments. Nonetheless, *Avnei Shoham* still feels Gentiles are prohibited from Shabbat and Torah Study. See R. Moshe Binyamin Tomashoff, *Avnei Shoham* section 1 page 19. The Radbaz seeks to clarify the discrepancy by saying it is a matter of intention: "A Gentile may only fulfill mitzvot for the sake of reward. He is forbidden to accept them as obligations incumbent upon him" (Touger, 604 n. 64.)

250 See Clorfene and Rogalsky, 41–42.

251 Exodus 13:9, 16, 31:13, 17; Deuteronomy 6:8–9, 11:18–20.

252 Adler, "The Sabbath Observing Gentile: Halakhic, Hashkafic and Liturgical Responses," 14–45. He also discusses Rashi's opinion that a *ger toshav* is required to keep Shabbat. This is based on Exodus 20:10, 23:12 and Deuteronomy 5:14 where a *ger* "stranger" is not to be made to work on Shabbat.

253 For what a Gentile Shabbat and Festival observance might look like according to one halachic authority, see Schwartz, 235–292.

254 *Responsa Egrot Moshe, Yore Deah* 2:7.

255 Schwartz, 255–256.

256 *Shoneh Halachot, siman* 304. Note that his statement is generally seen as offering *benei Noach* permission to keep the commandments but not necessarily encouraging them to do so.

257 Rabbi Michael Shelomo Bar-Ron, *Guide for the Noahide: A Complete Manual for Living by the Noahide Laws* (Springdale, AR: Lightcatcher Books, 2010), 4–5.

258 Bar-Ron, 164.

259 Bar-Ron, 162.

260 y.*Avodah Zarah* 2:1.

261 Matthew 28:19–20.

262 For a similar view in the *Didache* see Draper, 257–283.

263 Menachem Kellner, *Maimonides on Judaism and the Jewish People* (Albany, NY: State University of New York Press, 1991), 33–47.

264 Kellner, 34, 46.

265 Romans 3:2.

266 Exodus 12:19, 43–49; Leviticus 7:7; Leviticus 24:21–22; Numbers 9:14; Numbers 15:14–16, 28–29.

267 David L. Lieber, "Strangers and Gentiles," *Encyclopaedia Judaica* (2nd ed.) 19:241–242.

268 Milgrom, 402.

269 See, for example, *Special Laws* 1:308–309, where he quotes Deuteronomy 10:18.

270 Shaye J. D. Cohen, *The Beginnings of Jewishness* (Berkeley, CA: University of California Press, 1998), 121.

271 b.*Yevamot* 47b.

272 b.*Yevamot* 47b.

273 b.*Bechorot* 47a; b.*Yevamot* 22a, 48b, 62a, 97b.

274 Gerhard Friedrich, "προσηλυτος," *Theological Dictionary of the New Testament* 6:728.

275 In the nomenclature of the synagogue, proselytes are called "sons of Abraham."

276 Lancaster, *The Holy Epistle to the Galatians*, 235–237.

277 David Flusser, *The Sage from Galilee: Rediscovering Jesus' Genius* (Grand Rapids, MI: Eerdmans, 2007), 50